Primary School Management: Learning from Experience

Case studies by primary and middle school headteachers

LLEG
'O

ITHDRAWN

1 5 MAY 2022

Primary School Management: Learning from Experience

Case studies by primary and middle school headteachers

Eric Briault and Neville West

NFER-NELSON

Published by The NFER-NELSON Publishing Company Ltd.,
Darville House, 2 Oxford Road East, Windsor, Berkshire SL4 1DF, England.

First published 1990
© 1990, Eric Briault and Neville West
© For individual chapters remains with the copyright holders.

British Library Cataloguing in Publication Data
Primary school management: learning from experience: case studies by primary and middle school headteachers.
1. Great Britain. Primary schools. Management
I. Briault, Eric II. West, Neville
372.1200941

ISBN 0-7005-1252-7
ISBN 0-7005-1253-5 pbk

Phototypeset by David John Services Ltd, Maidenhead, Berks
Printed in Great Britain by
Dotesios Printers Ltd, Trowbridge, Wiltshire

Hardback:
ISBN 0 7005 1252 7
Code 8360 02 4

Paperback:
ISBN 0 7005 1253 5
Code 8361 02 4

Contents

Glossary of Terms

DES   Department of Education and Science.

ERA   Education Reform Act 1988.

ESL   English as a Second Language.

ESRC   Economic and Social Research Council. This body receives proposals for research and awards grants.

GRIDS   Guidelines for Review and Internal Development in Schools. Primary School Handbook. 2nd Edition by R. Abbott, S. Steadman and M. Birchenough, Longman for Schools Curriculum Development Committee 1988.

GRIST   Grant Related In-Service Training. A system of funding in service superseded by LEATGS (see below).

HMI   Her Majesty's Inspectorate. The Inspectorate is appointed primarily to give professional advice to the Secretary of State and Department of Education and Science. Their terms of appointment are to the Crown and they are independent of government.

INSET   In-Service Education and Training.

LEATGS   Local Education Authority Training Grants Scheme. Governed by the Education (Training Grants) Regulations 1987. This scheme requires each LEA to submit annually to the DES a plan indicating their planned expenditure and sum to be spent on national priority areas (NPAs) and local priority areas (LPAs). Many LEAs have devolved part of their training budget to schools.

LMS   Local Management of Schools. All secondary schools and primary schools with more than 200 on roll will have budgets delegated to them by April 1993. Headteachers and Governors will be responsible for the finance and resource management of their school under this system. The allocation of resources to individual schools has to conform to the formula which forms part of the Local Management Scheme which requires the approval of the Secretary of State.

NNEB   National Nursery Examination Board.

OTTO   One term training opportunity. This was a scheme to promote training whereby headteachers and teachers were released for a period of one term to engage in development programmes funded by central government and usually mounted under the auspices of institutions of higher education. Replaced in 1986 by GRIST (see above).

PTA   Parent-Teacher Association.

SFSD   School Focused Staff Development. This was the title of a collaborative project between East Sussex County Council and the University of Sussex funded by a grant from the ESRC (see above).

SPMG   Scottish Primary Maths Group. A commercially produced mathematics scheme for Infant and Primary Schools published by Heinemann Education.

Introduction to the Studies

Towards good management

The experience arising from our association with the management programmes provided by the Management and Professional Development Unit of the University of Sussex leads us to believe that a range of case studies written by Headteachers who have taken part in the programmes may serve to illuminate and inform the essential principles of the management role of a Primary School Headteacher. The programmes to which we principally refer are the One Term Training Opportunity (OTTO) initiatives, attended by experienced Heads, and the 20-day programmes designed by them as part of their full-time term release. Such programmes are now implemented under alternative funding, but the acronym 'OTTO' has been retained to denote the particular features of these programmes.

We have taken the view that the presentation of groups of case studies, together with commentaries upon each of the groups, would provide Primary School Headteachers and those preparing for headship with material likely to be directly relevant and useful to their role. The book is directly aimed at such a constituency, together with those engaged in headship management training and those professionally advising Heads and schools. We see also a body of useful material which might be drawn upon in training programmes for school governors.

A symposium in four sections

We therefore invited sixteen Heads to provide a case study based on their own experience, under one of four sections into which we have structured this symposium. Each invited Head received from us a brief under one of the following headings:

1. Improving the quality of pupils' learning experiences.
2. Staff organization and development.
3. Policy and the management of resources.
4. The head, the school and the community.

The headship role

In the introduction to each of these sections we give a short summary of the brief given to the Headteachers concerned and go on to indicate the themes of each of the four case studies. After each case study, we invite the reader to consider the wider implications of the study, its relevance to the reader's own circumstances and to the changing situation since the passing of the Education Reform Act (1988). To assist in such consideration, we offer a short comment and one or two possible questions which might be asked.

Following the studies in each section we offer a commentary intended not merely (or even mainly) to comment on the studies, but intended rather to seek to place the experience described in the broad context of our understanding of the essential nature of the headship role. Three themes underlie this understanding:

- The concept of leadership.
- The Head as manager.
- The changing relationship between those responsible for education in England and Wales.

The in-school leadership role

It may be agreed that there is a spectrum of leadership styles, frequently cited in management literature, ranging from the authoritarian through the consultative to the 'primus inter pares' stance. We would argue that it is inappropriate to define leadership in terms of particular traits. Effective leadership is more to do with the adoption of an appropriate leadership style given the context and the goal to be achieved. Equally, given that management is about the achievement of goals through other people, the leader needs to be aware of the degree of maturity of the individual concerned in relation to tasks to be undertaken. Typologies of leadership may, however, assist in the process of constructing a repertoire of styles appropriate to task and situation. In presenting this view we acknowledge the concept of situational leadership developed by Hersey and Blanchard (1982). It may well be the case that Heads as managers need to develop a capacity to move beyond their preferred leadership style. This will involve the Headteacher in a consideration of the weight and importance given to different aspects of leadership. How far does the leader seek to be recognized as being alongside his or her colleagues, supportive, friendly; how familiar does s/he aim to be with pupils? By what means does the Head, or the teacher, or the group exercising a leadership role convey to colleagues the wider view of the school as a whole? It remains the case that some teachers identify largely with the concerns of the children in their charge rather than with school-wide issues, being content to leave such matters to the Headteacher. In what circumstances and at what stage does a leader take the initiative, lead from the front and at the same time ensure that individual members of staff are not being left behind and failing to accept ownership of corporate goals?

The adoption of an appropriate leadership style is bound to involve a recognition of the range of knowledge and experience within the staff team in relation to particular goals. By what means is support and development aimed at improving teacher performance best achieved? In exceptional cases supportive action may fail in its purpose and serious weaknesses may persist: when does a supportive leadership style need to be replaced by one of critical assessment?

Several of the case studies describe action by the Headteachers exemplifying the leadership role and changes in that role in relation to developing circumstances; others less directly reflect some of the issues raised.

The Head as manager

We have found it helpful to make use of a sequence of management behaviour. This can usefully provide a checklist against which specific and personal experience may be assessed. The sequence, under five headings, may be outlined as follows:

1. *Aims and needs*

While it is arguable that logically an assessment of aims should precede the examination of needs, in practice consideration of aims and needs may well take place concurrently. The recognition of needs inadequately met may be the starting point for action; equally a reconsideration of aims may lead to a reassessment of those needs which it appears desirable to take into account. In defining educational aims, the person or group exercising managerial responsibility will wish to consider for whom and to whom they are responsible, since different needs may give rise to potential conflict. In resolving such matters, priorities and value judgements will have to be made.

2. *Briefing and consultation*

Acceptable decision-making depends upon adequate consultation, which in turn requires effective briefing of those consulted; the process of consultation may well reveal the need for fuller briefing. In the judgemental process that follows, what is to be the nature and extent of consultation? Who so far has considered aims and needs, who has assembled the necessary information – the Head alone, a small management team, an *ad hoc* working party? Whatever the answer, consultation is likely to be widened, values and priorities discussed, factors weighed. What degree of consensus is essential, how long a delay can be accepted in seeking to reach it, before a decision is made?

3. *Decisions*

The managerial decision to take specific action must cover the initiative itself – the new action – the nature and extent of delegated responsibility, and the specific arrangements for putting decisions into effect. Communication precedes action. Who needs to know? What form of communication is most likely to lead to the acceptance of responsibility for action?

4. *Implementation and monitoring*

At this stage, the managerial role becomes an executive one. The process of implementing decisions necessarily involves some observation of immediate outcomes and is likely to call for some degree of modification of original plans. Thus the recognition of the need for monitoring is an essential part of the process of implementation. Who is to make sure that the intended action actually takes place? How far does self-assessment prove effective in practice? By what means is the ultimately responsible manager or managerial group able to check whether or how far the decisions made are being implemented?

5. *Evaluation*

Intended outcomes are implicit in the stages leading up to decisions. Arrangements need to be made to gather evidence in order to make judgements about outcomes. These outcomes, some of which may have been unanticipated, are likely to lead to a reassessment of aims, a consideration of next steps, a review of each stage of managerial behaviour in respect to the particular enterprise undertaken.

We invite the reader of the studies and commentaries which follow to check how far the actions taken appear to have had regard to this management sequence. The comparatively small size of most Primary Schools and the absence of subject–departmental structures bring Headteachers into a particularly close relationship with their colleagues. Everyday contacts provide the answer to many of the questions raised but the possibility remains that some steps in the sequence may sometimes be less than fully considered.

Changing relationships

We have in the past recognized that at the national level, the distribution of powers and responsibilities between central government, Local Education Authority and schools forms what might be described as a triangle of tension. The Education (No. 2) Act 1986 and the Education Reform Act (1988) have changed the nature and extent of the powers held by the centre, the locality and the teachers. At the level of the individual school, these changes will radically alter the power/responsibility relationship between the Local Education Authority, the governing body and the Head and his or her staff. The introduction of the National Curriculum transfers powers formerly held, but not very much used, by the LEA (Local Education Authority) to central government and greatly reduces the opportunity for the individual school and teacher to determine the curriculum framework and broad content. While giving parents as a whole no powers over the curriculum, the reconstitution of the governing bodies gives the representative parent governors a much stronger opportunity to influence governing body decisions. The requirement under the 1986 Act for governors to report annually to parents may prove important in this connection. Governors' decisions in turn will, under the new Act, relate to a much wider range of powers and responsibilities than at present. The financial clauses in particular will result in a major shift from the LEA to the individual governing body. Alongside these statutory changes, the increased recognition by the educational professionals of the importance of parental cooperation and understanding, particularly at the primary school level, is resulting in significant initiatives.

Relations with the wider community

The attitudes of Headteachers towards parents, governors, LEA officers and advisers range across a wide spectrum, from a basically distant stance to one of maximizing involvement in ways which are consistent with the Head's contractual obligation to oversee the effective functioning of the school.

Relationships within the governing body are of particular interest, for on that body parents, teachers, elected members of the Authority or persons appointed by them, take part together in discussion of the school's affairs, in the presence of and often with participation by LEA officers and advisers. The co-options made to the new governing bodies under the 1986 Act should enlarge the opportunities for a variety of interests to be brought to bear. The Head/chairperson relationship is clearly an important one. What is the strength and nature of relations and communication between meetings of the Governing Body? What steps does the Head find it desirable and effective to take in order to give individual governors a fuller insight into the workings of the school?

Relations with parents as a whole are often largely to do with meeting informational needs, or providing explanations of practices within the school. How far beyond this might the Head go in practice? Is consultation with parents a reality in the sense that it can result in a change of plans or a reconsideration of existing arrangements at the school?

These questions are worth asking in relation to the experience described in our case studies and remain relevant since the Education Reform Act. But the Act will clearly bring about a major change in the school/LEA relationship and alter the Head/class teachers/governors relationships. With the concentration of power and responsibility within the school itself and under the governing body, these relationships are bound to develop in fresh ways.

These then are the themes which inform the case studies of this symposium together with the range of questions which are considered in the commentaries that follow them.

Section 1 Improving the Quality of Pupils' Learning Experience

Introduction

Contributors to this section were invited to focus on the curriculum-in-action in their schools and submit case studies which centred on initiatives relating to maximizing pupil progress and enhancing the quality of learning experiences offered to pupils. We asked contributors to acknowledge the distinction between the espoused curriculum of the guideline or other such documents formulated within the school and the curriculum-in-action experienced by pupils. We were interested therefore in how guidelines were constructed, or reviewed on the one hand, and how the Headteachers undertook the process of managing and monitoring the curriculum-in-action on the other. Given that management is about the achievement of goals through other individuals we were also interested in any instances of how Headteachers had engaged in this aspect of the management of change.

Study A

Study A provides a case study of how cooperative teaching was initiated and developed in a First School. The study outlines how the classroom autonomy of class-teachers came to be replaced with a cooperative culture, an exchange that had a marked effect on the quality of learning experiences offered to pupils. The value of a collegial approach to management was recognized during an OTTO programme and it was this aspect which provided the focus for development on the return to the school of the Headteacher concerned.

Study B

Improving the quality of learning experiences in the Mathematics curriculum provides the focus of this study. It traces the attempts made to bring about change, first by the adoption of a commercial Mathematics scheme throughout the school, and, following an inspection of the school by LEA inspectors, the role played by two further initiatives: focused visits to other schools to observe the Mathematics curriculum-in-action and the support role played by a newly appointed Deputy Head who also acted as a Mathematics consultant within the school. This study raises a number of issues concerning the management of change which are subsequently explored in the commentary.

Study C

This study outlines the strategies adopted by the Headteacher in seeking to improve and coordinate teaching and learning in Environmental Studies. As a consequence of his own participation in an action-oriented management course the Headteacher was convinced of the value of involving staff in the process of curriculum inquiry rather than the traditional top-down model of change. By doing so the Headteacher sought to bring about greater understanding of teaching and learning processes, and concomitant ownership of the process of change by the staff.

Study D

This study, like that of school B, outlines initiatives taken in relation to the Mathematics curriculum. The focus is upon the role played by a new Headteacher in managing and supporting the initiatives delegated to a senior member of staff, the latter's own learning on a 20-day course and their role in seeking to implement the recommendations of the Cockcroft Report. It portrays some of the anxieties experienced by a Headteacher deciding to increase the level of delegated authority and identifies some of the constraints on the action noted on the way.

Reference

COCKCROFT REPORT (1982). *Mathematics Counts*. London: HMSO.

Study A: Cooperative teaching

Background
School A is a First School with 360 pupils on roll located in a mixed catchment area. Children are drawn from both private and council housing estates.

Three years ago I was appointed to the headship of a first school in the suburbs of a southern town. The school has about 360 children, most of whom live in small privately owned homes. When I joined the school there were eleven classes; in my first year I appointed a Deputy and a probationer, to join the nine long-serving teachers. The main part of the school was built in the 1950s and consists of six classrooms, each opening onto a long corridor. Four of these rooms are linked in pairs. A scola unit has three further classrooms and a shared area. There is also a single and double temporary hut.

It took me much of the first year to settle in. During my second year I attended a 20-day management programme. This was an ideal time for such a programme of self-development; it enabled me to identify and evaluate management issues, formulate plans and devise strategies to implement change. The programme heightened my awareness of my own strengths and weaknesses in leadership and management, giving me confidence to work with staff in my own particular way.

Good practice

My initial evaluation of the school was of good practice throughout. Most of the children knew what they were doing, why they were doing it, and what they would do next. Most of the classrooms were attractively presented with relevant displays. The teachers were committed and hard working, friendly and open, and they welcomed and accepted the new staff. However, they worked in isolation. With the exception of the scola unit, where the Deputy worked, doors to adjacent rooms were kept shut. Year groups met, but only to identify the content of a shared topic which was then pursued separately in each classroom. During my first two years the open climate continued and developed. The staff gained confidence in my management and were receptive to new ideas.

Through my experiences in the management programme I became increasingly aware of the value of staff working together. They can share resources, ideas and skills. They can discuss problems, and colleagues can provide valuable support to resolve weaknesses. I believed that introducing cooperative teaching would improve the learning experiences for pupils, so I identified this as a goal to work towards with the staff. The start of a new school year provided the opportunity.

My first step was to discuss the idea with the Deputy during our weekly meetings, and over two or three meetings a plan was formulated. We planned to use the organization and location of the classes to create groupings of staff, and establish cooperative teaching. We limited the plan to the lower school so that we could select staff receptive to the idea, use rooms suited to cooperative teaching, and direct resources to support the plan. We hoped that the success of the work would encourage the other teachers to want to adopt cooperative teaching.

I identified five teachers willing to take the lower school age range, who had good relationships with each other and who would be open to the suggestion that they use cooperative teaching. I talked informally and individually to them about working together, and whom they might like to work with. I then allocated rooms, giving consideration both to their preferences and to groupings that I felt would best enable the plan to develop. The five were subdivided into a pair and a trio. In a double room were a long-serving teacher, enthusiastic and innovative, and the newest teacher, intelligent and well organized but still cautious. This partnership had complementary skills which would be mutually beneficial. The remaining three teachers would work in a double and adjacent single room. I hoped that they would gain from each other's particular strengths: Mathematics, language and Music. All the staff involved were good teachers, and I was confident that they would work at the task with a high degree of professionalism, but I was also aware that even apparently small changes can be threatening to staff, and I was anxious not to undermine either their confidence or goodwill.

Advantages of working together

During the Summer Term I spoke to the group about the advantages of working together. I suggested that in the double rooms the doors could be left open for most of the day, and that there should be some cooperation beyond agreement about the topic. As long as these quite limited requirements were fulfilled they were free to interpret cooperative teaching in their own way. I reassured them that they were to remain fully responsible for their own class in all areas of the curriculum and that I was proposing cooperative, not team teaching. They discussed the ideas as a group and as a pair and a trio, and reported back to me. All were very happy to try the plan. The trio decided to do music, TV, logic and stories together, and work separately for other activities. They would link with the pair for singing. The pair embraced the idea fully and seemed to spend every spare minute talking about it; plans changed daily. My advice was sought on some matters but I left the decisions to them. With all the group I was anxious that they should devise their own way of working, a way that they believed in, and could successfully implement.

In September the trio implemented their plan to work together. They worked willingly and cooperatively in planning and running activities, swapping children, rooms and resources as appropriate. But the doors in the double room were often closed. The teacher on one side was keen to have them open and sought my advice. The other said she wanted them shut because the children hadn't settled yet. When the partner opened the doors, equipment such as the TV or computer trolley was used to create a barrier. I considered the situation; the willing teacher was an excellent practitioner and would continue her good work whether the doors were open or shut. The other teacher seemed threatened. She had a lively class and perhaps felt inadequate by comparison with her colleague. I decided not to put pressure on the teachers to open the doors as the stress incurred might outweigh the advantages gained. All three continued to teach cooperatively the activities they had planned. The children gained by experiencing an extended range of music and logic activities. TV programmes were matched to groups rather than whole classes. Although I was aware that there was only limited cooperative teaching I commented favourably on the work they were doing and highlighted the benefits the children were getting. I hoped this would build the teachers' confidence in the concept of cooperative teaching so that they would continue to support its implementation. By the end of the year the trio had achieved part but not all of the goal.

In contrast the pair fully achieved the goal. They organized their double classroom together. The adjoining doors were kept open. New furniture allocated as shared items was jointly discussed and arranged. They shared imaginative play areas, and quiet work areas. Displays were planned and mounted together. Discussions about their work went on every lunchtime and evening, and I supported and helped them develop their activities. I made available weekly teaching time by a part-time teacher and myself, and ancillary help. This enabled a variety of teaching arrangements, and also demonstrated my enthusiasm for the work to other staff. I informally monitored progress by dropping in each week to work with the children, and would occasionally sit in on their after-school chats. I took every opportunity to comment favourably about their work to them. They talked with great enthusiasm to colleagues about the benefits of working together.

These two teachers and their children gained from the teaching organization. They made use of each other's strengths: one devised and organized various imaginative play activities for both classes, while the other planned creative writing activities to extend the abler children. They supported each other by sharing problems: the younger drew on the expertise of the other to help with slow learning children, while she in turn gave advice about the management of lively pupils. They exchanged ideas to create variety in repetitive consolidation activities. By pooling equipment they extended the resources available for logic work in each class. They made use of various organizational techniques: one would take 50 children for story while the other taught a small group. The teachers' development was evident. The younger teacher's caution relaxed. She would abandon a planned lesson to make use of an unexpected opportunity such as a snowy day. She gained confidence from successes such as an experiment with poetry writing with a small group, while her partner had the remainder of both classes. Her partner made a point of saying how much she too had gained from the pairing, but perhaps more importantly she saw the benefits to the children of working cooperatively. The quality of teaching and learning improved as the teachers drew on a wider range of teaching techniques and strategies to meet the variety of needs within the two classes.

Consolidating the change

The new academic year has brought new opportunities and challenges. Retirements and an increase in the staffing allocation have allowed the appointment of five new teachers, and all have been appointed with cooperative teaching in mind. Local Authority money for capital works will enable us to create new work areas that can be shared between classes. These changes will enable the expansion of cooperative teaching to most of the school, while the three teachers least confident with cooperative teaching can continue to work in individual class units in the huts. With more staff teaching cooperatively it has been necessary to devise a more formal organization to implement the work. Year leaders have taken on the responsibility of introducing and sustaining cooperative teaching within their year group. Job descriptions and the beginnings of a formal staff policy document, drawn up with the staff in the Summer Term, define and support the organization.

The new year is now half a term old. The building work is hardly started, but the new staff have settled in well. I am optimistic that cooperative teaching will be established in most of the school by the end of the year. The teachers are talking, sharing ideas, agreeing strategies, devising programmes of work, and using different methods of teaching and styles of organization. They are enjoying cooperative teaching. Throughout the school there is a feeling of togetherness, professionally and informally. I no longer see a need to direct all the planning myself; the teachers have taken ownership of the organization and are extending the degree of cooperative teaching within their year groups as they gain confidence. Most importantly I continue to see the improvement in the quality of learning experiences for the children that I first saw in the cooperative work of the pair last year.

Comment

Study A provides an interesting example of the sequence of management behaviour in action. It also demonstrates a Headteacher who adopted a leadership style appropriate to the situation in which change was intended:

- A good deal of attention was paid to assessing the situation, planning with the deputy and identifying different value positions and there was recognition of the paramount importance of retaining and extending teachers' confidence in their practice.

- The pace and scale of the change enabled those concerned to own the change and accept responsibility for their actions.

- The necessity to monitor change in a sensitive and supportive way was recognized.

- Consolidation was linked to organizational change, as indicated in the job description of year leaders and the expectation that they would continue to maintain the policy.

- The change was conceptualized as a learning situation for all concerned rather than a top-down model of change which runs the risk of token adoption.

Questions for the reader's consideration

- How might the Head best seek to extend cooperative teaching to the teachers in the hutted classrooms?

- How do we avoid or minimize discontinuity in a situation where buildings constrain a common approach to teaching?

Study B: Improving the quality of learning in Mathematics

Background
School B is a Group 6 JMI school with 410 pupils located in an outer London borough. The school site is comprised of two buildings, one dating from 1893 and three hutted classrooms. The main building, housing nine of the fourteen classes, has classrooms opening directly onto the main hall. The site is very cramped.

This study focuses on the changes which have taken place over the past two years, both in the basic management structure of the school and in the approaches to the teaching of Mathematics. Both changes were facilitated by the appointment of a new Deputy Head who has played a key role throughout what has been a most interesting and eventful period of development.

The school's management structure

Before the change, the senior management team comprised Head, Deputy, and Head of Infants – with the Deputy taking on the unofficial role of Head of Juniors. This meant that she coordinated the ordering and distribution of expendable stock for the juniors; organized playground and hall timetables; and carried out a number of other minor administrative functions which, although most important to the smooth running of the school, could in fact have been carried out by someone less experienced and well qualified. This I am sure is a familiar picture in many schools, but one which I would suggest probably constitutes a waste of a valuable human resource.

We now have an Infants Coordinator and a Junior Coordinator who, for their respective departments, carry out the whole range of administrative duties traditionally held to be the Deputy Head's domain. In addition to those duties already mentioned, the coordinators also regularly take assemblies and lead staff meetings; they tend to assume leading roles in most curriculum development, and they are generally perceived as 'extra deputy heads'.

All this, in turn, serves to release the Deputy, enabling him to carry out major management tasks which would normally be the prerogative of the Head alone – tasks such as the coordination of in-service training and other general aspects of staff development. This approach not only helps the professional development of the Deputy, but can obviously relieve the burden on the Head significantly – and I'm sure I'm not alone in finding it difficult to deal adequately with the myriad of initiatives regularly arriving on my desk.

In short, the new structure facilitated a far greater delegation of authority than had been possible hitherto, and it is becoming increasingly clear that the ability to delegate effectively will be a key management skill for all Heads faced in the years to come with the many and varied implications of the new legislation.

The antecedents to change
A few years ago, it is generally true to say that, in the junior part of the school at least, children tended to work through textbooks such as *Graded Arithmetic*, *Alpha* and *Beta*, and *Making Sure of Maths*, and that relatively little apparatus of any kind was used. What was taught throughout the school was predominantly arithmetic, often to the exclusion of many aspects of measurement and shape – and very little problem-solving and investigative work took place at all. Some of these things did, of course, happen but it was largely a matter of chance.

First attempt at change
In common with many schools at about that time, we undertook a major review of our Maths teaching and decided to adopt SPMG (Scottish Primary Mathematics Group) as our basic scheme in the belief that, with it, children could almost learn individually and at their own pace. A substantial amount of apparatus and equipment was bought, collected, or made; courses and meetings were attended by staff; and the Maths Advisory Team of the day were consulted and seemed in agreement with what we were trying to do. We saw no reason to believe that we were not on the right track...

Outcomes of change
Observation of classrooms and discussion with staff indicated that:

- children were now undoubtedly enjoying Mathematics, where before this had certainly not, generally, been the case;

- children were now learning Mathematics on a much broader base, with much more attention given to measurement and shape;

- much more apparatus of all kinds was now being used which was of particular benefit to those children of lesser ability who still needed this type of support well into the juniors; and

- teachers seemed more secure with the structure of a scheme to support them.

There were, however, in my view, other more worrying aspects to the changes:

- it seemed to me that the more able children were being held back by having to work too sequentially when they might have been able to take certain strategic short-cuts and still understand the concepts involved;

- it occurred to me, over a period of time, that teachers were not seen to be *teaching* as much as hitherto. In some classes it seemed that children were expected to learn for themselves from the books and materials, with, perhaps, inadequate guidance;

- some teachers were trying to teach individually which, with classes of 30 or more, was obviously unrealistic.

Most worrying of all, perhaps, was the perception of many parents, gained through the grapevine, that standards had fallen.

The second change attempt: curriculum review
And so to the past year which began with a new Deputy, who was also the new Maths curriculum leader, and with a complete review of the curriculum, a process which was coordinated by the Deputy.

To carry out the review, he used GRIDS (Guidelines for Review and Internal Development in Schools). This is a highly structured and comprehensive way of conducting a school review which centres around a survey sheet completed anonymously by the staff. In this way the staff as a whole are able to identify what *they* see as the principal strengths of the school and also those areas about which they are concerned and which therefore require development.

When the results of the survey are collated, two or three priority areas are identified which form the basis of planning such things as in-service training, deployment of resources, and the review of curriculum policies. The two major advantages of this system are, firstly, that there can be this concentration of energy into a limited number of agreed priority areas, rather than trying to do everything at once and not getting very far in anything; and secondly, because the staff themselves have determined the priorities rather than these having been imposed on them, they are much more likely to feel 'ownership' of subsequent development processes, and genuine change has a better chance of coming about.

The maths development plan

Fortuitously, Mathematics was quickly and easily identified as the main area of concern, and following structured brain-storming sessions we, as a staff, formulated a development plan. This targeted what we were actually going to do over the following two years in order to achieve the desired changes in the teaching and learning of Mathematics. In particular we looked forward to the production of a new policy document by the following Easter, which would appear initially in draft form following a series of staff meetings and workshops, and which would reflect consensus views throughout. This, again, was coordinated by the Deputy.

During our early sessions a number of initial areas of agreement emerged. We would retain SPMG as the core scheme, though much more supplementary material would be required; and we would need to standardize the way we used it. Practically everyone felt they needed a great deal of help, in terms of resources and advice, to introduce investigative Maths, problem-solving, and Maths games into the classroom. This was, in fact, where we started, and a series of after-school workshop sessions was arranged with the staff in two groups looking at either 'investigations' or 'games'.

The investigations group investigated and the games group played games, and invented and made some of their own, and, although not always to everyone's liking, 'putting yourself in the place of the children' proved a powerful learning experience.

From these sessions, packs of games, and ideas for others, were circulated to all staff, together with 'investigation packs' appropriate to each of the seven year groups in the school. I have seen a number of examples of these in use in classrooms and I know that the children thoroughly enjoy them and that staff regard them as useful and relevant. Furthermore, children have started taking investigations home which, apart from the obvious benefits, has proved a very valuable public relations exercise. The feedback from parents indicates that they are delighted to see how enjoyable their children find this sort of work, they are likely to recognize its value in developing worthwhile skills and concepts, and, of course, they often experience pleasure in helping with the problem at hand.

School inspection and response

Another major influence in the change process was the LEA inspection of the school in March.

One of the principal recommendations arising from our inspection was that we should adopt '. . .a system of planning based on expected learning outcomes'. This recommendation gave us considerable food for thought. Without clear guidance and effective working examples teachers may be overawed by such a prospect. We felt it sensible to proceed cautiously, and in the first instance proposed a system by which Mathematics could be planned for each class for each half term.

The use of forecast sheets has helped us to respond to inspectors' recommendations. Each teacher completes a sheet for each group within their class. Greater care in the selection of a limited number of topics to be covered and 'focused group teaching' have become two principles which we now employ. Focused group teaching is managed by carefully planning the work for the majority of the class so that the children will be unlikely to need attention. This leaves the teacher free to focus most of his or her teaching skills onto a relatively small group of children, and quality contact of this nature has proved most effective.

Arising logically from the forecast sheets were the review sheets, also to be completed half-termly. The first is used to identify intended learning outcomes and the topics concerned, the second to record the learning outcomes achieved by the pupils.

Staff visits to other schools

Another successful strategy to effect change has been a series of half-day visits arranged for all the staff to other local schools.

These visits were very carefully planned. The Deputy Head met the leader of the Maths Advisory Team and between them they paired our staff with teachers in other schools who were at a similar stage of development. We felt this was essential to avoid the pitfalls of teachers feeling their time had been wasted by having to visit someone from whom they had nothing to learn, or, perhaps worse still, being confronted by someone so good or different in style that they would be impossible to emulate.

In order to focus attention during the visits, the Deputy produced an observation form which could also be used to record findings and act as an *aide-mémoire* at a later staff meeting to discuss the visits.

Subsequent analysis and debriefing following such visits indicates that staff have found it interesting and stimulating and a rich source of new ideas. It has also proved a great confidence booster to discover that everyone else has problems and worries and shortcomings. It is a valuable ingredient when designing school-based INSET programmes.

Involving the parents

It is essential for parents to be fully informed of curriculum change within the school. We needed to gain feedback from parents: having expended considerable effort in managing the change, a change which had involved the staff in active learning, it was felt appropriate to involve the parents on similar lines – hence the Maths workshop for parents.

More than a hundred parents attended an evening session led by the leader of the Maths Advisory Team who explained how and why Maths teaching had changed over the years, and the importance of relevance. This was followed by the Head of Maths of a local high school explaining the implications of GCSE (General Certificate of Secondary Education) for the teaching of Maths at primary level. The parents were then invited to try out a whole range of Maths games and investigations which they tackled with relish.

Evaluating outcomes

As the period of planned change drew to a close, one important basic management task remained to be completed – that of evaluation – and one of my final tasks was to collate evaluation questionnaires completed by the staff to examine their perceptions of whether our work had been effective. The consensus was that this had, indeed, been the case. Staff felt more confident in their ability to manage their Maths teaching, they felt better equipped to cater for the needs of less able children and those with special talents, they felt more able to develop the basic competencies through investigative work and problem-solving, and the resource provision in Maths was felt to have increased significantly.

However, as always, none of this is important unless there has been an improvement in the quality of the children's learning experience. We are sure there has been, though this is difficult to assess accurately. Another set of data is that provided by objective testing. The Local Authority introduced assessment tests several years ago and our results in these indicate a definite improvement in Maths.

The role of the curriculum leader

A significant finding from the evaluation exercise was that the major factor in effecting change and development was felt to be the influence of the curriculum leader, and it must be said how useful it was that the curriculum leader in Mathematics was also the Deputy Head. It has always been my experience that most curriculum leaders, although well capable of working hard and producing discussion documents and other worthwhile literature, of attending courses and disseminating information, of performing a whole range of what might be termed non-provocative functions, nevertheless find it hard, if not impossible, to do or say anything that seems to place them in authority over their friends and colleagues. Now, this can be a major obstacle, especially when it comes to monitoring and evaluating – functions which can so easily be interpreted as being judgemental.

In our case, however, the Deputy Head has the authority, and, in any case, possessed the interpersonal skills to be perceived as generally non-threatening. He also had the time to concentrate his energies into developing a major area of the curriculum in this way, because of the quite radical changes in the school's management structure that took place on his arrival.

Before he came, our first attempt at change had lacked leadership and direction. Teachers were, in general, fed theory, given some new equipment and books and were expected to get on with it. Most were confused and felt insecure – some felt they were being de-skilled.

Since then change has been effective and relatively rapid, with review, followed by the formulation of a development plan, and a management structure which enabled the Deputy to become actively involved in leading the initiative, proving key factors.

Comment

Study B provides an interesting illustration of a Headteacher delegating authority to a curriculum leader who accepts the need to bring about change. In this case study we should note that the curriculum leader is also the newly appointed Deputy, who has the added advantage of positional authority to underpin his change-agent role. Delegation in itself is insufficient as a management strategy. For delegation to be effective the delegatee needs to have:

- appropriate experience;
- job knowledge;
- psychological maturity to undertake the task;
- willingness to accept responsibility for exercising authority;
- a range of strategies whereby they might meet the needs of different staff;
- awareness of the parameters of their authority;
- knowledge of how and when s/he is required to render an account for the decisions and action taken.

In this study we should note that formal review and the construction and implementation of a development plan were insufficient in themselves to meet all needs. An external inspection drew attention to learning outcomes, a need which was responded to constructively by the Head and Deputy. The school was a 'listening school' – a capacity which should not be underplayed.

Questions for the reader's consideration

- Given the requirements of the Education Reform Act, how might governors be involved in the process of curriculum change?

- How does a headteacher or headship team maintain its ability to respond to change when key members of staff leave the school?

Study C: Managing curriculum development in environmental studies
Curriculum review

Background
School C is an 8 to 12 Middle School with 400 pupils on roll and serves a mainly middle class catchment area in a pleasant country town in South East England.

During the Autumn Term the Deputy Head and I decided to make a systematic sample study of the work of the eight upper classes (the 11- and 12-year-old age groups). We looked at the work of two children in the lower, middle and upper ability range in each class. After initial discussions we decided to concentrate efforts for change on Environmental Studies.

There were considerable differences in the teaching strategies adopted by staff, extending from full investigative studies to dictated notes. In one class a child had written:

The body is compeaux machine which Requires constent Maintence. It must cleaned and feed, exirsised and carefully Maintain it needs warmth and oxgen to function correctly.

In one or two classes much of the writing was somewhat stereotyped and it was disappointing to see many missed opportunities for children to record personal reactions to the varied experiences they were being offered.

In other classes there was evidence of good personal writing, observational drawings carried out 'in the field', written accounts of interviews with adults and generally worthwhile investigative techniques. In talking to staff it was also clear that much oral work had been carried out.

There was little evidence to show any systematic development, or in some cases even acknowledgement, of the skills, concepts and attitudes as set out in the curriculum guidelines. We felt that there was generally an over-concentration upon factual material, which possibly revealed that some members of staff saw themselves as 'imparters of knowledge' rather than as 'facilitators of learning'. As a staff we were certainly not working as a team and as a consequence there was little continuity and little progression in the development of skills. It was also disappointing to find no records of detailed planning.

We both felt a strong temptation to rush in and attempt to put everything right in one go. This is, of course, a temptation to avoid at all costs although we did share some of our concerns with our colleagues. At this stage it was difficult to see ways of involving all members of staff since we were then in a period of national industrial action. We therefore decided to begin by developing a revised Environmental Studies scheme. We chose this area because not only is it of utmost importance in helping children to understand the world in which they live but also because it provides tremendous opportunities for the development and practice of a whole range of essential skills in almost every area of the curriculum.

Initial phase

In view of the fact that it was still not possible to arrange staff meetings we decided to set up a working party of Head, Deputies and the Environmental Studies and Science Coordinators. In time, as the industrial action lessened, this group was slightly enlarged. We set ourselves the task of establishing a new working document for later dissemination to the whole staff. During the Spring and Summer Terms we examined our 'aims and objectives', developed a list of skills and concepts and identified a range of attitudes and values we wished to foster. This also proved to be a good opportunity for us to review some of the current literature on the subject, particularly recent HMI documents.

Towards the end of the Summer Term we began to think about how we would disseminate our work to the whole staff. The main problem in the development of any area of the curriculum is to find ways of ensuring staff ownership. Unless staff feel that it is 'theirs' and they have a full understanding of all the issues it is most unlikely to achieve much in the way of change in the classroom. The process of policy formulation has long been regarded as being as important, if not more so, than any finished document.

During the Autumn Term, 1987, I began a full-time OTTO programme which necessitated my absence from school for the whole of that period and which also entailed a fairly high commitment of my time during the following Spring and Summer Terms. During the Autumn Term the Deputy had initiated the planned introduction to the Environmental Studies review. It was decided to use one of our five INSET days and to invite one of the County Inspectors to introduce and lead the day's activities. We had hoped to spend the greater part of the day in looking at our own environment and identifying possible starting points for investigative work with children. In the event, the staff were asked to look at a completely different area some miles away. Even though the evaluation of the day's work revealed the development of some negative attitudes, the exercise was, nevertheless, useful in identifying the processes involved in this kind of activity. It has, however, confirmed in my own mind the need to manage such activities with great care, particularly in defining both the task and the brief for both the staff and the guest leader.

Projects proposed

The area around the school is rich in environmental features and many starting points may be found. The village itself grew from a population of 1400 in the mid-1800s, to something over 15,000 today. As well as all the usual features there is a disused canal, now dry in parts, and a disused railway track. The whole area provides a rich source of worthwhile first-hand experiences.

It is planned to build up a series of projects which involve children in real investigations. The study of distant places and distant times can prove to be somewhat difficult with primary children: it is difficult to find real evidence and provide real opportunities when studying Australia, for example. We hope to overcome this problem by identifying occasions in the study of the locality that would naturally lead us further afield. The study of the disused railway line for example, might lead us to a study of the development of the national network. This study of distant times and places will take place over limited periods of time but will provide opportunities for the continued development of research and mapping skills, using both documentary evidence when available and reference books.

Teaching style

We are now at the stage when staff are about to explore our own locality, identify starting points and propose project headings for each year. Once this has been done we shall need to look at the overall balance between the various types of experiences offered, whether mainly geographical or mainly historical and identify how the various investigations will provide opportunities for the development of specific skills. Crucial to the whole of our future progress is the question of how the philosophy of individual members of staff is to be developed. However detailed are the plans for each proposed project they are bound to fail if staff still regard their prime function as imparting knowledge. Indeed, it is unlikely that the projects will be suitably planned unless teachers are able to focus on:

1. what kinds of experience will form the basis of the work;
2. how children will be led towards posing their own questions for investigation;
3. how the information will be gathered and used;
4. how conclusions will be drawn;
5. how the results may be communicated to others.

At the heart of these issues are questions relating to how children learn and how we see our role as teachers. Teachers who have always concentrated on what they do in the classroom rather than what the children do and who may never have experienced the organization of real, active learning experiences for children, have the 'furthest to travel'.

Perhaps the most useful introduction is for the teacher to experience the actual process for him or herself. Certainly most Environmental Studies courses currently on offer set out to provide an opportunity for an investigative approach and to build upon that enquiry to form the principles which underpin our work. At the moment we do have an opportunity to join three or four other schools for an in-service day along these lines. It is not unusual to find that the teachers who most need such an experience are often the most hesitant in putting their names forward and much encouragement may be needed.

Since the introduction of teachers' Conditions of Employment it is possible to arrange more staff meetings than was the case previously and these meetings will undoubtedly provide a valuable opportunity for further work. It is important that the process of formulating a new policy, in any area, should be an enjoyable one for staff; active learning is not just for children!

Since my engagement in the OTTO programme I am now convinced that teachers' experience of actual engagement in real investigations needs to go alongside policy formulation. In this way, the teachers' investigation becomes a vehicle for looking at both the process of investigation and more importantly the process of planning an investigation. The earlier plan to hold a series of discussions in order to examine the document produced by the working party has now been abandoned.

The revised project

We have decided to develop our work using the disused canal as a focus for raising issues. The process will involve several stages. In the first activity several sets of pictures and photographs have been prepared showing the canal as it used to be and what it looks like today. Working in groups the staff will be asked to raise questions about the canal. This activity has already been carried out with a group of children and it will be interesting for staff to compare the two. During the second session we shall be seeking to identify which questions require more than a simple factual answer; these are the questions which would give real purpose to an investigation and lead on to a consideration of a possible conceptual framework. For example, 'When was the canal built?' is not the same kind of question as 'Why did the canal stop being used?'. Hopefully, the latter question would lead into the concepts of 'change' and 'cause and effect'.

During subsequent meetings we shall be asking staff to look at a variety of documentary evidence, including copies of actual financial returns, Census material, posters and notices, written accounts and so on. These will be used to identify a range of possible activities which could be undertaken by children. We would then need to identify which skills would be developed in each of the activities. Unlike many present patterns we would only identify our aims and objectives towards the end of our investigation when, hopefully, we shall all have a better understanding of what is both possible and desirable. Obviously, at this point it will be necessary to look at published accounts of Environment Studies planning in order to enhance this part of our work.

By working in this way it is hoped to bring the abstract nature of curriculum planning closer to the process we shall actually use in our classroom teaching.

Looking to the future

At a later stage, when staff have been out 'into the field' and identified possible 'year' topics the curriculum coordinator will undertake an overall review to ensure that we reach a balance between the historical, geographical and scientific elements of our work. Having once established the overall pattern of the topics detailed plans will be developed for each one. This, together with the development of resources and the formulation of means of evaluation, is a considerable task and can only be achieved with a good deal of team work. At each stage of the more detailed planning we shall need to ensure that we are maintaining both progression and continuity.

Hopefully, by engaging in the task in this way, members of staff will not only gain greater ownership but also become more prepared to reveal uncertainties and difficulties, and thus the needs for future in-service work will be identified.

If we are able to manage our curriculum planning and delivery in this way, I am hopeful that we shall considerably enhance the quality of the children's learning experiences. Keeping careful records of our planning should certainly make life easier for new members of staff or for members of staff moving to different year-groups. As yet, we have not identified all the strategies the curriculum leader will use in monitoring the new curriculum 'in action', but if we are to maintain our policy this will be an essential task for the future.

It seems to me that working from a consideration of the resources at hand avoids the pitfall of planning a project that has little or no chance of being implemented in accordance with those principles of learning which we believe should form the basis of all our work.

Comment

The effectiveness of the change strategy reported here is the consequence of conceptual-izing change as a learning process, rather than being achieved by stressing dissemination of a policy few would share. Such a process takes time but it is time well spent. The common ground between teacher and pupil is that of a shared learning experience. By engaging in the learning process staff became familiar with the same processes they would expect their pupils to engage in. The strategy shifts the emphasis away from teaching (the initial problem) to that of learning. As the Head states: 'Those who may never have experienced active learning may have further to travel'. Only *after* immersion in the learning process did the staff address the issue of aims and objectives, and only then did published accounts of practice become relevant. Having shared experiences together the coordinator then focused attention on the need for balance, on the need for methods of assessment and evaluation.

So far they have not decided on strategies for monitoring the new approaches. This is a critically important element in the management of policy implementation. Policy for teaching and learning is observable as it surfaces in the classrooms of individual teachers. Each teacher engages in his/her interpretation of the policy. It is this that makes the monitoring process so important and why the monitoring process is again a learning opportunity for all involved. Effective monitoring is in one important sense equivalent to effective learning. Ownership of a policy for teaching and learning is not achieved at the outset, it is achieved through the process of development-in-use of new ideas.

Until that stage is reached we can only ever say that policy has been *affirmed*. Monitoring, and the dialogue generated through the monitoring process, enables the manager to establish an agreed range of practice and at the same time safeguard continuity, progression and balance in the curriculum. Monitoring helps to achieve a better match between the 'public map' of the policy document and the 'private image' of classroom practice.

Questions for the reader's consideration

- How far do you feel that active learning is a constructive strategy to use when seeking to introduce changes associated with the national curriculum?
- What would you identify as the key features of the monitoring process?

Study D: A new headteacher and the planning of change
The need for change

Background
Housed in a post-war, two storey building, school D is a Group 4 Junior school serving an owner-occupier residential area in a London Borough.

I was appointed Head Teacher of a Group 4 Junior school serving an owner-occupier residential area in the South East during the late 1980s. It was my first headship and I was soon aware that parental expectations were high, and tended towards a model of education that could loosely be called 'traditional'. Mathematics, regarded very firmly as one of the 'basics', had its progress largely measured by ticks against sums. However, the Mathematics policy document I inherited had spoken of 'a lively, enjoyable and active interest in Mathematics for its own sake', 'the expression of creativity', 'aesthetic value', 'pattern', 'predictions of outcome' and so on, all of which provided evidence of some thought being given to the Mathematics curriculum. Nevertheless, there appeared to be some mis-match between the school document and what could be observed as a working philosophy in the school.

This mismatch stemmed very largely from the dissatisfaction staff were feeling with the Nuffield Mathematics which had recently been introduced, following discussions between the staffs of the Junior School and the attached Infant School. A general inspection of both schools had stressed the need for attention to be paid to continuity from one to the other, and a scheme common to both was seen as a major contribution to that continuity. However, signals I was receiving from my colleagues suggested that they were unhappy with the Nuffield Scheme.

Generating and stabilizing staff confidence

From the outset the Scale 3 Mathematics Coordinator, who also had responsibility for Science, kept closely in touch with me, reporting feedback he was getting about Mathematics in the school in general and their dissatisfaction with Nuffield in particular. Our discussions led me to the view that the introduction, let alone the implementation, of a newly thought out school Mathematics policy should not be hurried, for three reasons. First, the staff needed to develop confidence in their Mathematics teaching following the unsettled feeling they were experiencing as a result of adopting Nuffield Mathematics and the comments of the Mathematics Inspector. Second, I felt the Maths Coordinator himself needed time to develop his own confidence in working with his colleagues. Maths was a new responsibility for him, and it was clear that he himself needed guidance and training. Third, and possibly most important, I myself was new to the headship. The school had passed through a difficult stage, and I saw my initial task very much one of stabilizing colleagues' confidence in me and with each other, and securing for the school a sense of purpose and acceptance of the need for development.

Notwithstanding the importance staff attached to the notion of continuity between the Infant and Junior schools, I believe they perceived their own autonomy to be under threat. What seemed to be lacking was any real sense of ownership by the staff of the problem of improving continuity in the Maths curriculum. My suggestion that we explore the possibility of adopting an alternative Maths scheme might seem to have been rather too direct, but it did give us a common feeling of purpose, and it did address the misgivings staff felt over the use of Nuffield, which appeared to lack depth, particularly for older and abler pupils, and was short on extension materials.

Establishing relationships with the advisory service

Chief among the schemes we explored was SPMG (Scottish Primary Maths Group, a published scheme). The coordinator played a valuable role in discussing our moves with the local authority Maths advisory team, and the feedback he received from them was that SPMG might well meet our needs. It was from this point that the coordinator began to develop a close relationship with the advisory team, and I encouraged this. He spent a great deal of time visiting them at the teacher's centre, and made known to them the current school situation.

Involving the governors and the feeder school

From the outset I advised the governors of our thinking, and they expressed concern about the transition from the Infant to the Junior school. As a result of this concern a meeting was convened by the school's attached Inspector, attended by myself, the Head of the Infant School, the Maths Adviser, and the Inspector himself. A frank exchange of views took place, and I made it clear that we wished to proceed with SPMG as a first step in developing our Maths work throughout the school. The adviser endorsed my view, and general agreement was reached that Nuffield was an excellent scheme for the Infant School, and provided a firm conceptual base for the Junior School's maths in which SPMG would have an appropriate part to play. It was also agreed that a statement should be prepared on behalf of both schools and the following statement was presented to the governors of both schools:

> Following discussions it has been agreed that the Junior and Infant schools should work together in formulating a set of aims and objectives common to both schools. It is understood that in the pursuance of these aims a wide variety of resource material will be used reflecting the differing needs of the schools and the individual children, but that a rationale of concept-based, practical and investigative Mathematics will be in the forefront of our approach to teaching.

Strategies for change

My task as I now saw it was to set up strategies for the effective development of Mathematics, starting with the drafting of a set of aims. A top-down model of management was clearly inappropriate: I wanted members of staff to have time to get to grips with ideas which were in accord with some of the notions of Maths stated in the policy documents as they then stood, and I was not in a hurry to produce new documentation. There was a clear role here for the Maths Coordinator, but he did need some input of his own to help him get his ideas across to his colleagues. He also needed more time since he had responsibility for Science as well as Maths.

Linking Maths and science initiatives

The arrival of a new Deputy Head whose main curriculum interest was Science provided the opportunity for the Deputy and Maths Coordinator to work together in developing good practice. As the Cockcroft Report points out, 'there is a great deal of overlap between practical mathematics and science in the primary years and many activities could take place under either heading' (paragraph 327). A period of effective school-based in-service training was planned. The Deputy Head instituted a series of sessions with her colleagues, for which I relieved her of class teaching once a week for one hour. She also assumed a strong management role in encouraging and advising her colleagues in many aspects of school practice. She gave valuable support to the Maths Coordinator, but I was still anxious that his own insights into good practice and the coordinator's role needed development. When the possibility arose of his attending a 20-day course for Maths Coordinators, I made strong representations to the Maths Inspector, and secured his membership on the course. An important element on the course was the requirement to work with colleagues in the classroom.

There were thus school-based in-service initiatives in two linked curriculum areas (Maths and Science) with the result that colleagues began to relinquish some of their classroom autonomy. Ideas were shared and there was an increased willingness to display a variety of mathematics work. Above all, the nature and purpose of children's work in Maths was subject to greater critical attention, with more stress being placed on investigatorial and open-ended activities.

Extending the coordinator's role: whole-school involvement

During the Summer Term the coordinator extended his management role by planning his programme and convening his own curriculum development meetings with the staff. My own role here was one of encouragement and support, but I asked for a log to be kept of the term's initiatives. By the end of the term the coordinator's role had become more clearly defined and he was applying it with greater vigour. Some important developments had taken place: one initiative is worth recording. Following a suggestion from the Maths Adviser that the whole school might consider pursuing one topic in order to bring into focus their thinking about the *aims* of maths, the coordinator led a programme in which the whole school explored triangles.

Work displayed provoked reaction from teachers who were surprised by the variety of work; although an agreed set of aims was not formulated, staff were becoming less dependent on the published materials. Most importantly, the staff had been actively engaged in monitoring the curriculum-in-action. Barriers were beginning to be broken down, ideas were shared, and teaching styles discussed. Teachers were engaged in a valuable process of self-evaluation – a significant stage in staff and curriculum development.

Organizational change

When the time came for organizing classes for the new academic year, I asked the Deputy Head and Maths Coordinator to take charge of the two first-year classes. There seemed to me to be several points in favour of this move.

1. They had developed a professional relationship in the development of their respective curriculum areas and would make a good year group/class–teacher team.

2. They would have greater opportunity to plan and work together, both as curriculum leaders and as class teachers.

3. The Deputy Head would be able to ultilize her management role to good effect.

4. The development of shared aspects of Maths and Science would be on a secure footing.

5. All the various efforts at improving school practice, and matching that practice with *notions* of an effective curriculum, would develop upwards from the first year. In other words, good practice could be established from the moment children entered the junior school.

INSET and resources

As part of our INSET budget for mathematics training, the two second-year class teachers have attended two one-day courses; and their use of investigational work has increased accordingly. It is part of the general heightening of awareness going on throughout the school. A set of aims for the school has now been drawn up and a document prepared outlining the use of apparatus in the school, together with lists of apparatus considered essential for each classroom. Current resourcing is meeting this particular need, and a great deal of mathematics equipment and materials have already been purchased for the school's central stock. As yet, we have no up-to-date policy document outlining objectives; but our shared understanding has grown and provides a reference point for further work. We recognize that the 'broadening of the curriculum has had a beneficial effect both in improving children's attitudes to mathematics and also in laying the foundations of better understanding' (Cockcroft Report, paragraph 286).

Outcomes

It is difficult to gauge how our pupils' progress has improved. Attitudes are more positive, the work more varied, the sense of commitment and persistence greater. We have not fully addressed the notions of independent and cooperative working espoused in *Mathematics from 5 to 16*, but our pupils have gained in confidence, as have the teachers. Mathematics is now much more than a school subject. Children, individually or in groups, are using their skills purposefully. Fourth-year children helped to design the newly installed pond, from working out the optimum size to provide easy and safe access for a class of 30 children, to calculating the area of butyl liner and volume of sand needed, together with the relevant costings. We have much to do, but the mystique has gone. Mathematics has acquired a human face, and it is frequently smiling. We are much more able to meet the requirements placed upon us by the National Curriculum.

Comment

In this study the Head effectively manages the concern a leader must have for the welfare and development of personal relationships on the one hand and concern for task accomplishment on the other. Awareness of the need to exercise leadership in a number of different arenas is also evident in the study. Not only is there concern for the task; there is concern for such stakeholders as governors, the feeder school Headteacher and attached Inspector. Heads will increasingly have to engage in transactions across the boundary of the school as the move towards local management of school proceeds. Delegation of authority was viewed as desirable but was deferred until the coordinator's task maturity increased by involvement in a 20-day training programme. After such training the psychological maturity factors were constructively supported by the joint involvement of the Deputy Head and Maths Coordinator. The leadership style was proactive, anticipatory and founded in careful analysis of needs.

Whilst there is citation of changed attitudes on behalf of pupils and a greater willingness on the part of staff, such developments will need careful monitoring if the dynamism of change is to be sustained. The location of both change agents in the first-year classes is clearly an investment strategy.

As in Study B, the decision has been made to defer policy formulation until staff have assimilated the values and process which underpin the changes. The construction of a policy for mathematics should not be deferred for too long, for it could be a positive means of maintaining the dynamism referred to earlier.

Questions for the reader's consideration

- The Head identifies five reasons for locating the Science and Maths Coordinators in the two first-year classes. What alternatives to such a course of action can you identify? On what grounds?

- The Headteacher asked the Maths Coordinator to keep a log of initiatives taken during the term. How would you follow up this initiative, which was designed 'to encourage and support'?

Commentary on case studies A to D

The Headteacher as the chief executive of the school is centrally concerned with the identification of needs and the management of change within the school. The four studies reported in Section 1 illuminate contemporary issues relating to the management of change which will be explored in this commentary. In seeking to promote curriculum change that addresses the issues of continuity, consistency, balance and coherence (GB. DES, 1985) the Headteacher is obliged to consider a number of questions:

- How much variation in curriculum practice (what teachers do in classrooms) is permissible if such criteria are to remain meaningful?

- In what ways will information on such features be gathered within the school?

- What are the professionally acceptable means of monitoring the curriculum in action that also promote imaginative rather than defensive responses and encourage innovative activity within the school?

Whilst primary Headteachers have traditionally played a significant role as change agents and have engaged in unobtrusive monitoring of the daily life of their schools, the features of the contemporary curriculum are such that no one person can now deal with the range of issues likely to be identified across the curriculum as a whole. In Studies A to D the Headteachers delegated particular stages to individual teachers, rejecting top-down approaches in favour of strategies which increased the likelihood of staff accepting ownership of the intended change.

The problem-solving approach

This involvement of the whole staff, or significant sub-groups of staff, in a problem-solving approach to change requires the Headteacher to accommodate two conflicting tendencies within the Primary School system. Under one approach to management the response to problems arising within the school is accomplished by the formation of teams or groups of individuals with the appropriate expertise, experience and task maturity to tackle the problem, after which the team disbands. Requisite authority is delegated to the group, which is given access to resources and deemed to be accountable to their colleagues for the action taken. The promotion of such a task-based approach (or task culture) requires the head to effectively negotiate and communicate a working brief, clarify terms of reference and identify the level of decision-making the group is empowered to make. It is equally important for the Head to communicate such details to the rest of the staff and publicly legitimize such work. Such an approach requires teachers to forgo some of their classroom autonomy in exchange for opportunities to engage in decision-making at the level of the school.

In contrast, a role culture is premised on the notion of expert knowledge linked to role differentiation, whereby teachers take on particular responsibilities in addition to their role as classroom teachers. Such responsibilities are increasingly being set out in written job descriptions. Since the Primary Survey of 1978, which reasserted the need for scale post-holders to have more impact in their schools, Headteachers have been increasingly obliged to endorse the process of role differentiation by identifying members of staff who act as consultants in the various curriculum areas. Under the restructuring of teacher salaries such differentiation applies to teachers on the Main Professional Grade and is developed further in schools large enough to qualify for Incentive Allowances. The match between expert knowledge required in a particular curriculum area and the possession of such knowledge and experience by the teacher charged with responsibility for a consultancy role is notoriously difficult to accomplish, a fact which is often ignored in references to the work of curriculum consultants in the Primary School. Within schools this mis-match is rarely a subject for discussion since it is tacitly accepted by members of staff; at best the system works on the principle of 'best fit'. The primary Headteacher is obliged to manage the process of change in the light of such tacit knowledge. Study B illustrates the sense of relief experienced by the Headteacher when he had available the happy coincidence of expert knowledge and experience combined with the positional authority of Deputy Head. Such matters are not trivial; they shape the alternatives available to a Headteacher in managing the process of change. The strategy of consultants offering support and guidance when requested by their colleagues is characteristic of many Primary Schools. Shifts away from such responsive/reciprocal styles of consultant behaviour to forms which are more participative or seemingly interventionist will take time to accomplish. There are signs that such changes are taking place (see Campbell, 1985 for example). The Select Committee (1986) clearly endorsed a Primary School culture in which 'virtually all primary school teachers should combine roles of classteacher and coordinator in particular aspects of the school's (or group of schools) work' (ILEA, 1985). In the four studies, consultants were involved in the formulation of initial plans by inclusion in the 'inner cabinet' of Head and Deputy. But, as the process of managing the change proceeded, either all the staff or groups of staff became involved in collective enquiries of some kind. Where consultancies exist in token form it is likely that the individuals concerned will become marginalized or ignored.

Mismatching of guideline and action

Each of the studies acknowledges the mismatch which existed between the espoused curriculum of the guideline and the characteristics of the curriculum in action. All four Heads demonstrate their awareness of the inherent weaknesses of a top-down approach to change, and in studies C and D it is also acknowledged that the adoption of a new commercially produced Maths scheme (SPMG, 1978) did not bring about the envisaged changes. The adoption of the scheme was not matched with appropriate adaptation of existing practice. Resource-based change is an attractive option, but, as acknowledged in studies C and D, it also requires teachers to examine very fully the implications that adoption has for their existing classroom practice. Having identified the changes in classroom practice that adoption requires it is then necessary to provide time and support to enable staff to acquire the appropriate skills and understandings.

Ideally, monitoring and reflecting on the characteristics of the current curriculum should engage teachers themselves in action learning. This strategy was employed in each of the studies reported here. What is particularly noteworthy is that in each case the process of policy formulation was deferred to a later stage when such a policy was more likely to reflect understandings gained through critical analysis of current practice, or practical investigations relating to the proposed change. Tackled this way a policy statement on teaching and learning is more likely to mirror practice and inform future decisions about practice than would be the case if policy was drawn up *ab initio*. Investigations in studies B, C and D involved staff in workshops in which they engaged in the learning modes being proposed for the children. Most people acquire new insights through action learning of this kind. Teachers came to understand Environmental Studies more fully by engaging in such work, became more confident about investigative approaches in Mathematics by undertaking problem-solving activities in a supportive, non-threatening climate. Such approaches take time but, as one contributor states, such shared activity helps to 'create a climate in which individuals may change themselves'. Many innovations have more to do with changes in the value systems of the individuals concerned than with the acquisition of wholly new skills. Changing existing values is the key which opens the door of change, and in Studies A and C the Headteachers gave a great deal of attention to this aspect. It takes time for staff to say openly 'Can we say what we really feel?' Openness in discussion, the acceptance of the searching question and the admission of uncertainty are all signs of the process of change proceeding at an appropriate rate for the individuals concerned.

In the brave new world beyond the Education Reform Act, matters relating to the content of the curriculum have been settled largely by procedures subsumed under the Act, but the field of curriculum practice continues to be presided over by the profession. In a climate of increasing accountability it will be necessary for schools to demonstrate their willingness to engage in monitoring and apply appropriate forms of evaluation to the curriculum-in-action. There is little doubt that evaluation will become a key component skill of headship. One arena for evaluation is the classroom itself where data is gained by means of participative or non-participative observation. Many teachers find such a prospect highly threatening. The Education Reform Act has left the field of classroom practice to the profession. Primary teachers lay claim to professional status on the grounds of their pedagogic expertise. This being so, it would be illogical for them to resist classroom observation, which in any case will be central to it. The management skills of the Headteacher are crucial here, for it is not sufficient to make observation palatable; the process of enquiry has to be managed and coordinated in a way that promotes growth and development, and leads to the solution of problems. Managed effectively it can provide a means of establishing norms of collegial enquiry aimed at improving the quality of learning experiences offered to pupils. It offers the prospect of task-focused groups engaging in critical reflection on matters of practice in ways that illuminate and inform rather than observation premised on imported models of teacher performance. Whilst classroom observation is currently a problematic area it is in any case one element in the process of teacher appraisal that now forms part of every teacher's conditions of service. It is clear from the Steering Group Report based on the six Appraisal projects sponsored by the DES (Department of Education and Science) that observation is acceptable to teachers provided that it is cast in a developmental rather than punitive or narrowly accountable light. This is well indicated in case study F in Section 2. Focusing on learning outcomes, as shown in Study B, and the importance of staff cooperation is demonstrated in each of the four studies.

Classroom observation was not employed in Study C but the sampling of pupil work from each of the classes in the school provided a starting point for Head and Deputy. Systematic sampling is an under-used approach to monitoring. Provided that staff understand the purpose of the exercise and the criteria for the analysis are made clear such an approach has much to commend it, indeed there is no reason why members of staff should not be involved in this process. Where this has been tried the teachers concerned have found it particularly valuable to see work across the range of classes within the school, which puts the work of their own class in context. To employ such approaches, norms of individual teacher autonomy first have to be changed. The studies in Section 1 indicate how four Headteachers engaged in that process in their schools.

Keeping parents informed

Each of the studies demonstrates the importance of keeping parents informed of the changes taking place within the school. In each case communication took place after the implementation stage, either through whole-school meetings/workshops for parents or through meetings called by class-teachers for the parents of pupils in their class. In two cases staff from the secondary school also endorsed the changes, reflecting not only a concern for continuity between schools but also helping to assuage lingering parental doubts. Given the changes in the patterns of involvement by parents and governors in the management of schools it will increasingly be the case that consultation will take place before the decision is made to proceed with the change. Such a process of consultation is not a simple matter, particularly in situations where the parents may hold traditional views on matters of classroom practice. In any case there is always a degree of uncertainty about outcomes at the beginning of a new initiative, when alternatives are imprecisely mapped out and staff are to be engaged in a process of critical reflection. This uncertainty is prone to be interpreted as 'wooliness' by parents who prefer to trade in certitude. The earlier parents and governors are brought into the counsultation process the more important it becomes for Headteachers to be clear about the purposes served by such meetings, to communicate these to parents, and at the same time pay particular attention to how the case for change will be presented to a lay audience without implying criticism of current practice in the school.

In each of the studies the teachers were being asked to consider and agree on how teaching and learning should be characterized in different areas of the curriculum. In Study B consideration of concepts, knowledge, skills and attitudes provided a matrix for guiding action. Involvement in action provided opportunities to allay anxieties and explore conflicting values. None of the studies attempted a prescriptive approach to matters of practice, but each of them attempted to identify the principles which should underpin and characterize classroom work in the curriculum areas concerned or, as in Study A, how teachers should cooperate. In this way it became possible to establish the range of acceptable practice in the areas concerned without being oppressively prescriptive. The strategy of establishing pooled resources for learning through collective action gives everyone a stake in the enterprise.

Curriculum change takes far more time to achieve than is generally acknowledged. It came as no surprise that these studies cover substantial periods of time. The school of the 1990s will have to be increasingly sensitive to the views of the consumers of the educational enterprise, to involve them in the process of change and increasingly construe them as resources in the process rather than audiences to be converted. Each of these studies recognizes the centrality of the teacher in the change process, the usefulness of collaborative approaches to school improvement and the ultimate goal of implanting inquiry as an ongoing process in the school. These are major targets of organizational development and will thus take time and resources to achieve. Those schools who have moved in this direction will find their response to the National Curriculum much more easily managed.

References

CAMPBELL, R.J. (1985). *Developing the Primary School Curriculum*. Eastbourne: Holt, Rinehart and Winston. London: W.B. Saunders.

EDUCATION, SCIENCE AND ARTS COMMITTEE (1986). *Achievement in Primary Schools, Vol I*. London: HMSO.

GREAT BRITAIN. DEPARTMENT OF EDUCATION AND SCIENCE (1978). *Primary Education in England*.

GREAT BRITAIN. DEPARTMENT OF EDUCATION AND SCIENCE (1985). *The Curriculum from 5 to 16*.

INNER LONDON EDUCATION AUTHORITY (1985). *Improving Primary Schools*. London: ILEA.

SCOTTISH PRIMARY MATHS GROUP (1978). Published Maths Scheme. London: Heinemann Educational.

Diagram 1:
MATHEMATICS DEVELOPMENT PLAN

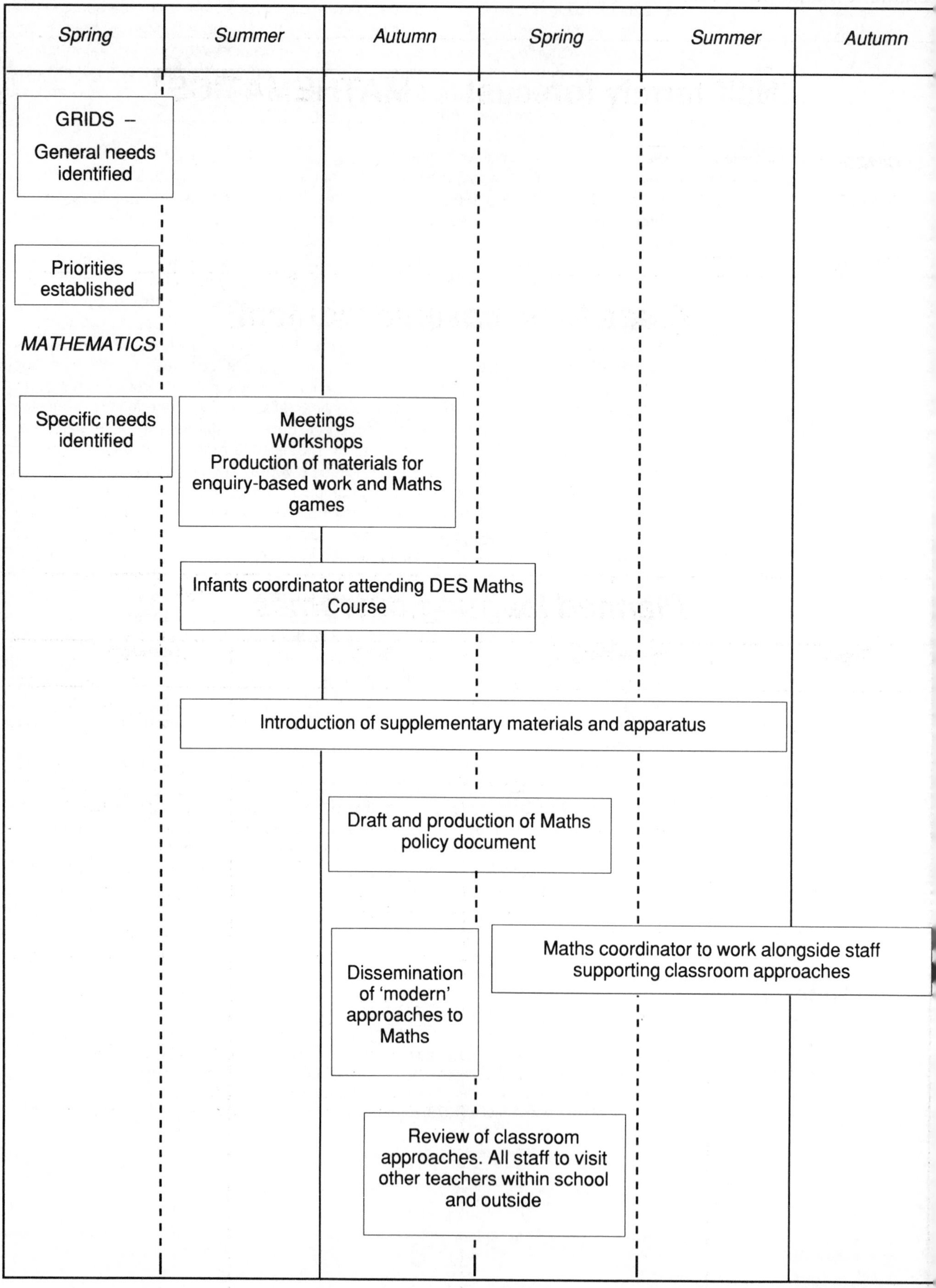

Spring	Summer	Autumn	Spring	Summer	Autumn
GRIDS – General needs identified					
Priorities established					
MATHEMATICS					
Specific needs identified	Meetings Workshops Production of materials for enquiry-based work and Maths games				
	Infants coordinator attending DES Maths Course				
	Introduction of supplementary materials and apparatus				
		Draft and production of Maths policy document			
		Dissemination of 'modern' approaches to Maths	Maths coordinator to work alongside staff supporting classroom approaches		
		Review of classroom approaches. All staff to visit other teachers within school and outside			

Diagram 2:
TEACHERS' FORECAST SHEET

Half-termly forecast   MATHEMATICS

CLASS					
GROUP	1	2	3	4	5

DATES: From   To

Areas to be covered (content)

Planned learning outcomes

Topic	Knowledge	Skills	Concepts

Diagram 3:
STAFF VISITS TO OTHER SCHOOLS

Mathematics development plan
Half-day school visits

Name ....   Date of visit ....

(A) *General*

School visited: Age group of class:
Core commercial scheme:
Other resources used:
Are resources stored centrally?
What methods of planning/recording take
    place in Maths?:

(B) *Classroom based*

How is the classroom organized?

How is the Maths equipment stored?

Is it easily accessible for the children?

How much balance is there between the six teaching styles described
    in paragraph 243 (Cockcroft Report)?

Is there a definite Maths area?

Is there a Maths-based display?

How are the children grouped?

Is all the children's Mathematics commercial-scheme based? If not what
    other resources are being used?

Are calculators/microcomputers actively promoted in the learning of Mathematics?

Are the children encouraged to use practical apparatus? If so in what ways?

Diagram 3: (cont'd)

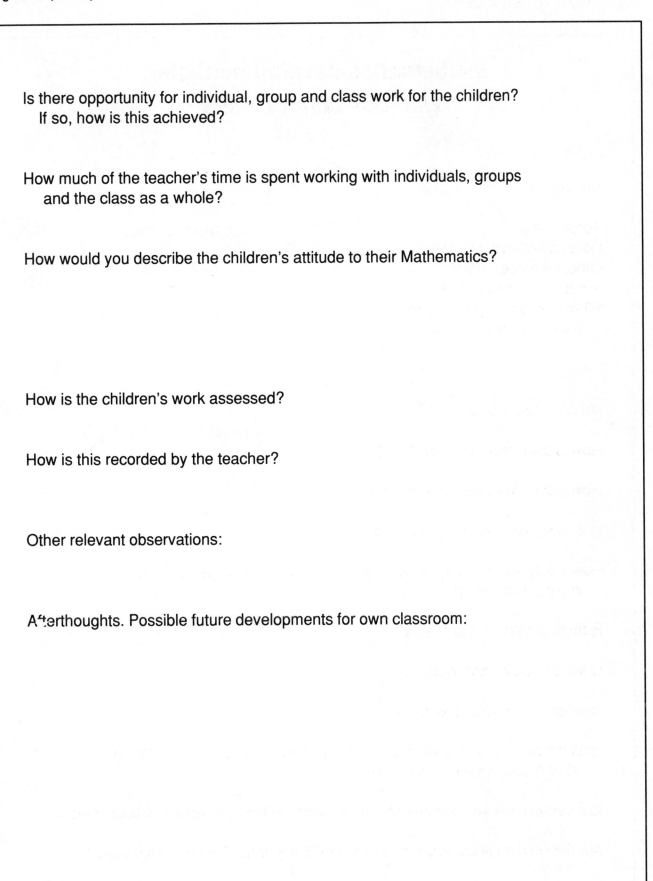

Is there opportunity for individual, group and class work for the children?
   If so, how is this achieved?

How much of the teacher's time is spent working with individuals, groups
   and the class as a whole?

How would you describe the children's attitude to their Mathematics?

How is the children's work assessed?

How is this recorded by the teacher?

Other relevant observations:

Afterthoughts. Possible future developments for own classroom:

Diagram 3: (cont'd)

Section 2 Staff Organization and Development

Introduction

We asked contributors to this section to address the following questions:

- How can Headteachers organize their school and devolve responsibilities to make best use of the talents of staff and sustain morale and commitment?

- How might the Headteacher best promote the continuing professional and personal development of staff and support them in their longer-term career aspirations?

- How might a staff development policy ensure sufficient commitment to the continued improvement of classroom practice?

Currently there are movements towards more careful analysis of teachers' strengths and potential, to the identification of unmet needs, to the formulation of policies aimed at maximizing individual growth, and to the construction of school development plans to achieve corporate goals (Thomas Report, 1985). New initiatives in Primary Schools have to be accomplished in a work setting that is sometimes characterized by teacher autonomy, and where staff carrying particular responsibilities must gain the cooperation of others over whom they have little, if any, formal authority. The requirements of the Education Reform Act are placing new demands upon schools and provoking the need for changes in the organizational culture of schools. That is one reason why schools are finding the changes more difficult and complex than hitherto.

The financing of school development plans has been assisted through In-Service Training funds deployed to the school under the LEA Training Grant Scheme started in 1987 (GB.DES, 1986). The DES Note of November 1987 (GB. DES, 1987) makes clear the role to be played by institutions and Local Education Authorities (LEAs) in the matters relating to the evaluation and monitoring of training needs and programmes. The combination of such initiatives, outlined in Circulars and Notes, together with the Education Act of 1988 provides a model of controlled decentralization by which the school remains accountable to central authority for the manner in which resources are deployed in pursuit of goals given priority by the DES. Decisions on how such goals are to be achieved remains the province of the school in conjunction with its governing body. The introduction of Local Financial Management schemes continues apace and longer-term plans have to be cognizant of the increased autonomy which schools will take on. This financial aspect is dealt with in Section 3.

Each of the initiatives described by contributors in this section took place against this background of administrative and legislative change. Two of the studies outline initiatives taken in one LEA that has established a policy of school-focused staff development which will be applied to all Primary Schools in the LEA by September 1989. The process of staff development aims to bring about an appropriate and effective organizational culture in which Headteachers make best use of the talents of staff and maintain commitment to an agreed vision of the school. Contributors were asked to outline the ways in which they identified and promoted the talents of staff and how they managed the interplay between their concern for people (sentience) and their concern to achieve corporate goals (tasks), and how they constructed appropriate organizational structures within their schools. By 'structure' we mean the deliberate patterning of relationships created to bring about the achievement of goals. Primary Schools have been characterized as institutions which are 'organizationally flat' since few intermediate positions of authority exist between Headteacher and staff who, in any case, spend virtually the whole of their time in teaching a class of pupils. This characteristic is one of the important ways in which Primary Schools differ from Secondary Schools. Such features present a challenge to Headteachers wishing to facilitate the process of staff development. Staff development is seen here as an active process in which individuals are given opportunities to extend existing skills and understandings or to develop fresh insights into the key components of their role. Managed with sensitivity the process enables both personal development and the achievement of corporate goals.

Study E   This study outlines how, as a consequence of involvement in a funded project the principle of school-focused staff development was introduced to the school and subsequently developed over an extended period of time. The study pays attention to the problems which arise after the initial innovatory impetus and the key role played by the Headteacher in this process.

Study F   Study F provides an example of how a school-based project undertaken on an award bearing course came to have real consequences for the school in the context of staff development. The study outlines problems met with during implementation of 'mutual observation' and the value of starting from open-ended, teacher-defined purposes as a means of gaining acceptance of the process in the school.

Study G   This case study outlines attempts made to re-energize a school caught in the downward spiral of a falling roll. Attempts at curriculum review were only partially successful. The decision to inform parents more fully about the curriculum-in-action received the support of staff. The part played by a curriculum newsletter prepared by year groups within the school is outlined, together with the effects this has had on forward planning, improved record keeping and curriculum review.

Study H   Study H outlines how the concept of a Planned Developmental Opportunity (PDO), introduced on a management programme, was applied and explored by the Headteacher. The study explores the value of this approach by considering the processes involved from the perspective of Head and Deputy, together with the response of staff to the initiative. This approach involves the Headteacher in the identification of skills, knowledge and insights likely to be acquired in the prospective PDO, the construction of a brief and the setting of short, medium, and longer-term targets. Central to the notion of such an opportunity for a Deputy Head is the assumption that headship is best conceptualized as a partnership in which Head and Deputy refine, each in the other, the skills of critical reflection on the process of management.

References

GREAT BRITAIN. DEPARTMENT OF EDUCATION AND SCIENCE (August 1986). Circular 6/86. *Local Education Authority Training Grants Scheme*. London: HMSO.

GREAT BRITAIN. DEPARTMENT OF EDUCATION AND SCIENCE (November 1987). Circular 14/77. *Survey of Arrangements concerning the School Curriculum made by LEAs*. London: HMSO.

INNER LONDON EDUCATION AUTHORITY (1985). *Improving Primary Schools*, Report of the Committee on Primary Education, Chaired by Norman Thomas.

WEST, N.F. (1987). 'Planned Development Opportunities in the Primary School' – mimeo. Brighton: University of Sussex.

Study E: School-focused staff development

Background
School E is a JMI school serving a community on the edge of an expanding country town in South-east England.

The project

My awareness of School Focused Staff Development (SFSD) came about when I was invited to join a pilot group of ten representatives from seven schools (four primary, three secondary) with two course directors and a course coordinator – set up to launch a Sussex University LEA project on SFSD, funded by the Economic and Social Research Council (ESRC). This involved a one-term secondment which started with a study of work undertaken in other parts of the country and which gave us a good foundation on which to base our efforts. It soon became clear that a considerable amount of staff development work was taking place at the school but that it had not been identified as such and was largely based on the way my own role had developed within the school. This had not only benefited the school's Deputy Headteachers (four appointed to headships in a ten-year period) with whom I worked closely, but rubbed off on other colleagues with three Deputy Headships, three Scale 3 promotions and a number of other steps forward being achieved in the same period. Promotion is, of course, only one small way of measuring staff development. Much more is gained through increased involvement in the running of the school and through additional challenges. As my role and management style changed, so did the roles and opportunities of those around me.

The management style of the Headteacher

At the start of my headship career I adopted a formal, traditional and somewhat autocratic approach. Following experience of headship my style has evolved to become far more open and based on trust and consultation. I now know that the presence of an open style of management contributed significantly to the success of the SFSD work and gave a thrust to the shared management practices I now enjoy within my school. The need for a more consultative, democratic approach should be recognized. Other colleagues – and not only Deputies – have the right to opportunities to enable them to play more meaningful roles in the management of schools. Not to do so is to waste untapped talent, to ignore the professional development of staff, and to serve injustice on the pupils who eventually benefit from the process. I have concluded, therefore, that the attitude of the Headteacher is crucial to the success of any SFSD scheme.

Demands upon schools

Demands upon schools have increased dramatically in the 1980s and will continue to do so into the next decade. Heads are now managers of educational establishments with more than curriculum-based responsibilities to handle. Increased personnel, public relations, new relations with governors, financial, administrative and organizational aspects of the role have added to the already considerable pressures, taking Headteachers further away from their traditional teaching roles. Many Headteachers are resisting this trend, stating that they weren't appointed to handle accounts or public relations, and so on. The new challenges cannot be met by Headteachers alone, the managerial role must be shared. The emancipation of the Deputy Head could be one of the positive benefits from this process. This is an obvious outlet for Headteachers, but requires a recognition of the Deputy Head as a joint manager (if not quite an equal) who can share the load and contribute considerably to the effective management of the school. It is hoped that Deputy Heads will rise to such opportunities. This collegial approach to management cannot occur overnight but it can be promoted by the establishment of a staff development policy within the school. The creation of such a policy will involve others in decision-making processes and create opportunities for involvement in school affairs. An appropriate staffing structure is important here.

Establishing a staffing structure

Before the start of the SFSD project I had developed a staffing structure as a consequence of a series of staff meetings in which frank views were exchanged. At the request of staff and in consultation with the Deputy Head a list of curriculum/organizational tasks was completed. The tasks were aimed at improving the effectiveness of our work with pupils. In circulating the list I suggested that staff should indicate three areas that interested them or which they felt they could fulfil. This formed the basis for the negotiation of tasks and particular roles to particular staff. A period of time was agreed in which staff could adapt to their new roles. This was to be followed by the introduction of job descriptions. It was at this point that the school became involved in the school focused staff development project.

Communication is a key element in staff selection. It was important that staff were aware of the concerns of the project and my part in it during my release time at the university. Bulletins provided one means of doing so, together with staff discussions during my school-based days of the project. The need to develop the staffing structure further by gaining agreement on job descriptions provided a useful starting point and led to the discussion of broader issues relating to staff development.

The staff development questionnaire

After the periods of discussion with individual members of staff there came the need to gather further data. This was obtained by means of the questionnaire to staff, a copy of which is included at the end of this study.

Analysis of the replies formed the basis for our draft SFSD policy which was eventually endorsed by members of staff. The LEA were able to fund release time to enable staff interviews to take place in school time. Agreement was gained from staff to include staff review or appraisal as an element of our policy. The agenda for such reviews were agreed together with the framework by which Headteacher reviews would be undertaken.

The effects of expanding the staffing structure

The SFSD Policy that emerged from this process was fairly comprehensive and its programme for the year ahead, together with the expansion of the staff structure and implementation of job descriptions, led us into a streamlining of an already effective school operation. All found their roles rewarding, and for some, the experience proved to be an awakening process, bringing out hitherto unused powers of organization and initiative. The change was very noticeable and colleagues were obviously pleased to be fulfilling roles beyond the demands of normal classroom routines. Special interest groups after school in various subject areas, organizing and hosting curriculum days, entertaining some of our many visitors, writing curriculum reports for governors, speaking at governors meetings, contributing to our in-house publication 'Curriculum News', acting as subject coordinators working alongside colleagues to set them an example or give them a lead, were some of the changes introduced. This brought closer involvement with school management and made individuals realize that they had much to offer the school in a broader sense and that they were capable of carrying additional responsibilities. The whole process has also brought tremendous development for me as Head of the school.

Management meetings

The introduction of management meetings, usually held once each month, was one important change. These involved a group of four: Head, Deputy Head, Head of Infants and Head of Juniors departments. A simple pattern was adopted for each meeting with each member of the group having the opportunity to speak on any topic. This could include the programme ahead (normal events and new initiatives), departmental problems, current work of special interest, staff problems and so on. Colleagues were encouraged to respond to the comments made and problems posed. This gave senior staff experience of management work and immediately improved the policy decision-making process of the school — four heads are better than one. I remember feeling 'good' after the first such meeting, the load had been shared and ideas came out that I might not have thought of in the same time span. Why hadn't I created such a group before? Was it the fear of sharing the responsibilities or an unwillingness to relinquish some of the power? Whatever the reason, I regretted not having done so years before. Following the meetings some items would go forward for further discussion at a full staff meeting or colleagues were charged with putting decisions into action, thus filling out their roles.

Resource implications

The opening up of senior roles that followed presented some problems because of the lack of time, the old enemy. Colleagues needed time within the working day to exercise their roles to good effect. A decision was made to reorganize timetabling and resources to enable the three senior colleagues to operate a 0.9 timetable, giving each one session when they could be about the school helping or advising colleagues in their day-to-day work. In time, the individuals concerned and the staff in general came to value this contribution greatly. The time allowed (0.1) is, of course, totally inadequate for the tasks involved and should only be seen as a gesture in the right direction. The total resource in this exercise (0.3 of full time) was simply taken from one provision to create another and was not additional time granted to the school. This highlights the need to re-assess existing practices whenever new initiatives are being considered. This release time is difficult to achieve in the Primary School and much more could be achieved with quite a modest improvement in the staffing ratio. Primary Schools should be placed on a more equitable footing with their Secondary School counterparts.

Staff review interviews

The development of roles, the facilitating of individual needs, and a greater appreciation of the individual's contribution to the life of the school was focused sharply through the inclusion of staff review interviews as part of our SFSD Policy. All agreed to take part and had been involved in the establishment of the agreed processes, yet when the time finally arrived all experienced considerable apprehension. Reassurance was very necessary together with a reminder that we were exploring the way forward together.

We had accepted that all should start their reviews with the same basic agenda and that the Headteacher should conduct the review interviews. Preparation on the part of the reviewer was of paramount importance to ensure the flow of discussion during each review. Interviews varied in length from 35 to 140 minutes.

All colleagues felt that the exercise was worthwhile and the overall view can be summed up by the comment of one colleague: '...My review lasted for two hours twenty minutes and I have nothing but praise for it. I was able to speak frankly and discuss my work of the past year and my aims for the future. During the normal course of events, this is not always possible'. The written summary of each review was prepared in the days that followed and once approved by both parties was signed, each retaining a copy for future reference. Confidentiality restricted the information to the parties concerned. The whole process was very time consuming. The interviews were held during the school day with time bought through SFSD project funds. This helped, but the review process makes considerable demands on the Headteacher and in large schools it would be necessary for senior staff to share this load. Much however will depend on the trust and confidence the teacher has in the person conducting the interview.

Headteacher review

Although the staff did not expect it, I arranged for my own review to be the first in the cycle. This was important to me as I was able to show confidence in the process and lead by example. My first review involved two of my staff – selected by secret ballot – and a primary adviser. A Scale 1 teacher from the Infants department and a Scale 2 teacher from the junior department were selected. The review was based on my lengthy job description. I found the exercise interesting and rewarding and being the first, it gave me a full understanding of the apprehension others were to feel and subsequently helped me to help others cope with it. Having used this pattern I am now looking to expand the process because in its present form it does not cover the full range of Headteacher responsibilities, since it is based on the perspectives of staff. Although this is very important and must remain part of the process, it is not enough. The Headteacher's role involves LEA, parents, governors, non-teaching staff, finance, public relations and so on. All must eventually find a place in the Head's accountability. The problem is, how can such a broad area be covered and by whom? Advisers? Peer groups? Governors?

The manpower implications of staff review are considerable and many recommendations have been made by different internal groups. A county working party recommended the appointment of additional advisers. Another suggestion has been the use of peer appraisal in which three Heads are each in turn reviewed by the other two. Teachers want Heads to be reviewed as often as they are. Review by governors alone is entirely doubtful given their lack of expertise and competence in this area. I believe that teachers should always play a part in the Headteacher review process. Linking school review to Headteacher review might be one way forward since the two are closely related. This might take place every four years and be followed by interim annual reviews related to agreed targets, this would of course require the appointment of additional advisers.

The effects of SFSD

The impact of our SFSD policy within the school was sharp and clear. Colleagues *did* become more effective as their roles were stretched, enabling them to show their full potential. The knock-on effect to the pupils was equally clear as the range and quality of curriculum work improved. The SFSD work had been developed with a very good team of teachers and based on a foundation of established relationships.

Some problems did arise, however, starting an 'application virus' of epidemic proportions. Once one colleague was successful in obtaining a post another applied. The end result was that in a period of eighteen months thirteen staff took other posts. The school had been used to, and indeed encouraged, the regular movement of staff, but the loss of so many, including some key personnel, in such a short time provided an enormous challenge for those who remained. The framework of our SFSD Policy helped us through this period.

SFSD and new appointments

All candidates shortlisted for appointments are sent copies of the SFSD Policy. Acceptance of the policy is expected of those appointed. The presence of a firm staff structure backed by meaningful, negotiable Job Descriptions has been of tremendous value, presenting those appointed with a firm framework from which to launch their roles. The heavier-than-usual turnover of staff meant that almost all those involved in the creation of SFSD Policy had departed, and the ownership aspect and the foundations on which it had been based, had been almost lost. A process of re-selling SFSD and of re-building trust and confidence was initially necessary and a fall back to the *ad hoc* Headteacher-guided approach prevailed for a time until these goals were achieved. Those appointed, of course, wanted to work at the school and were, therefore, eager to respond in a positive way. This period of re establishment is just ending and the new team, potentially stronger than the original team, is beginning to move forward with confidence. This re-building period was, I think, helped by the fact that everyone, everywhere, was taking stock of their situations because of the new Pay and Conditions of Service for Teachers. All that has previously been described – effective staff structure, open style of management, a SFSD Policy, and so on – helped us to move quite quickly, resulting in an accepted revision of the structure in keeping with the new Conditions of Service backed by re-negotiated Job Descriptions. The years ahead look promising.

Comment	The changing scene in school management requires more effective training for tomorrow's Headteachers/managers. SFSD is one way of enabling such developments, but schools will require INSET resources to help meet identified needs.

The work of the SFSD Pilot Group was taken on board by the LEA as county policy. The expansion of LEATG (Local Education Authority Training Grant) funding for INSET (In-Service Education and Training) and the need for forward planning and development plans has broadened the meaning of staff development, with policies becoming the vehicles for implementing wider plans. The creation of a school-focused staff development policy helps Headteachers to identify the needs of staff and at the same time promote whole-school improvement. A major outcome of SFSD should be an improvement in the quality of learning experiences offered to pupils.

Question for the reader's consideration

- Staff review, to be effective, needs to be supported by information gathered from a range of different sources. What types of information do you feel should be made available to the process of review?

- Development is a process, not an event. How does a Head avoid the review procedure becoming an annual ritual?

- If review interviews are confidentially based how does a Head make use of information made available to her which could assist in developments at whole-school level?

Study E: Staff development questionnaire

In the Bulletins circulated, I have tried to give a background on School-Focused Staff Development and an indication of its possible value in schools. I now plan to produce a *Draft Policy Document for Staff Development* and seek your help through completion of a questionnaire.

It will be helpful if completed questionnaires could be returned to my tray by Thursday, May 23rd.

So as to gain as wide a view as possible, it would be helpful if you *do not discuss your answers with colleagues beforehand* so that you give an individual response.

Your replies will be confidential, you need not identify yourself, and you can if you wish have your completed questionnaire back after collation. Your replies will only be used by me. You will be given a survey of the results. Your comments will not be binding in any way, but will simply reflect your views at this time.

Please be as open, honest and frank as possible in your replies.

I understand the pressures on your time and want you to know that your help will be valuable and much appreciated.

---

1. Assuming the need for a Staff Development Policy, do you agree   Yes/No
    that the aim should be to improve the quality of education for
    our children through improved development opportunities for staff?

2. Can you think of any other aims?   Yes/No
    If Yes – please specify.

3. Do you think that a School Staff Development Policy must be wide,   Yes/No
    so as to provide a source of help/offer opportunities for ALL
    members of staff?

4. Do you think that in formulating/operating a Staff Development Policy:
    (a) all the staff should be involved throughout
    (b) a representative group should be involved reporting back
        to the staff
    (c) only the Headteacher should be involved?
    (d) some other comment – please specify.

5. Do you think that visits to other schools are of value in our   Yes/No
    development?

6. Should we include a facility for arranging visits to other schools?   Yes/No

7. If you visited another school, what would you especially want
    to see?

8. Is there any value in arranging a class exchange facility in   Yes/No
    our Policy? (i.e. lower infants to upper juniors for a day, etc.)

9. Would you wish to take advantage of such an arrangement?   Yes/No/
                                                                Possibly

10. Would you value an opportunity to become a pupil for a day?   Yes/No/
                                                                   Possibly

11. Do you think that making a forecast for Project Work   Yes/No
    (flow diagram, etc.) is of value in your work?

12. Why is this forecast of value?

13. Do you set yourself other targets or goals in your work?   Yes/No

14. If 'Yes' please illustrate some targets you set.
    short term:

    long term:

15. Can you see any merit in extending this goal/target setting idea?   Yes/No

16. Do you agree with the need for job descriptions?   Yes/No

17. Job descriptions should be reviewed: (a) termly (b) annually
    (c) infrequently (d) bi-annually (e) as needs arise

18. Do you find your 'staff role' at the school challenging?   Yes/No/
                                                                Sometimes

19. Do you feel you have talents that are not currently valued   Valued
    or used?   Yes/No
                                                                 Used
                                                                    Yes/No

20. Should colleagues' responsibilities be changed from time to time   Yes/No/
    as the needs of the school/individuals change?   Possibly

21. When involved in applying for posts in other schools, would you:
    (a) value a source of advice in completing application forms
    (b) value advice in writing letters of application
    (c) value an opportunity for a 'mock' interview
    (d) value advice on the sort of post to apply for?

22. Do you think enough is done at school to fulfil your career   Yes/No
    development? (any comments)

23. How would you measure your current use of In-Service Training?
    (a) frequent use   (2–3 or more courses a term)
    (b) above average use   (1–2 courses a term)
    (c) infrequent use   (1–2 courses a year)
    (d) under-used   (1 course every two years or less).

24. Have you considered applying for DES Courses? (short)   Yes/No

25. Have you considered applying for Secondment? (long courses)   Yes/No

26. Do you feel our 'follow up' system to DES Courses through   Yes/No
    the production of Discussion Papers for staff is of value to the
    school?

27. How should applications for places on DES long/short courses
    be considered?
    (a) on an individual basis – individual shows interest,
        chooses course.
    (b) on a school planned basis – school chooses courses
        according to need, staff approached to apply.
    (c) a combination of (a) and (b).

28. Do you think that in general you are adequately informed of
    developments at school in:
    (a) general matters/organization, etc.   Yes/No
    (b) curriculum matters   Yes/No
    (c) external matters   Yes/No

29. Are there any areas in which you think you should receive more   Yes/No
    information?
    If 'Yes', please specify.

30. How would you describe the present style of school management?
    (Tick one or more)
    (a) open (b) consultative (c) democratic
    (d) autocratic (e) none of these
    Any comments:

31. Do you think more delegation in decision-making is necessary?   Yes/No

32. Would you like to see a change in management style?   Yes/No
    If 'Yes', please specify:

33. What do you dislike most about your job?

34. What do you dislike most about the school?

35. What do you like most about the school?

36. If you were now changing schools, and had a completely free choice, would you choose (a) an open plan school (b) a closed plan school?

37. Do you feel you have enough opportunity to express your views on Yes/No School Policy?

38. Do we have enough Staff Meetings?   (a) business meetings   Yes/No
                                   (b) curriculum meetings   Yes/No

39. Should we have a more planned programme for Curriculum   Yes/No
Staff Meetings? If 'Yes' should we meet
(a) as needed – present policy (b) once a month
(c) once a half term (d) once a term

40. Would you value the introduction of 'Special Interest   Yes/No
Group' Meetings to promote certain areas of skill?
(computers/pottery, etc.)

41. In view of the pressures on lunchtimes, should all our staff meetings Yes/No
be after school (say 3.30 p.m. – 4.30 p.m.)?

42. Would you accept meetings at 8.00 a.m. to 9.00 a.m.?   Yes/No

43. Do you prefer our present arrangement to 42 or 43?   Yes/No
(business at lunchtime, curriculum after school)

44. In recent times we have reviewed the curriculum in Mathematics, English, Religious Education and will shortly look at Science. What areas should we look at in 1985/86? *Tick 3* – add others if you wish.
    (a) Computers in Education   (g) Health Education
    (b) Art and Craft Work   (h) Staff Development
    (c) Social Studies   (i) Safety at School
    (d) Record Keeping   (j) General Review
    (e) Environmental Science   ....
    (f) Physical Education   ....

45. Do you see a need for working parties to be set up from time to   Yes/No
time to look into specific matters, reporting back to the full
staff meeting?

46. If a Review Interview System were to be introduced as part of an overall Staff Development Policy, do you think it would enable you to: (tick as necessary)
    (a) look at your own performance in the classroom
    (b) have an opportunity to state what you would like to happen/have
       to improve your work
    (c) develop your career prospects
    (d) review your effectiveness in your areas of responsibility
    (e) review your targets or agreed targets for the previous year
    (f) set targets for the next year?
    (g) What else?

47. Would you support the introduction of an Annual Review   Yes/No/
Interview as part of a full Staff Development Policy?   I need to
                                                      know more

48. Would you in principle, support/value an appraisal process   Yes/No/
as part of an overall, full Staff Development Policy with   I need to
the view to it forming an integrated/natural part of the   know more
school's programme?

49. If an appraisal system were introduced would you want it to be:
    (a) part of an on-going review of work, drawn together at   Yes/No
       an informal interview?
    (b) a two-way process with appraisee and appraiser   Yes/No
       contributing?
    (c) considered a constructive process in your professional   Yes/No
       development?

50. Would you support such an appraisal scheme *as part of* an   Yes/No
Annual Review?

51. How often should review/appraisal interviews take place?
(a) twice yearly (b) annually (c) bi-annually (d) other?
(*Assuming all appraisal interviews would follow a set pattern.*)

52. Would you want any appraisal conducted by:
(a) an internal source (b) an external source?

53. Assuming adequate training was given to those involved in carrying out
appraisal, would you prefer such work conducted by:
(a) Headmaster (b) Deputy Headteacher (c) adviser
(d) a senior colleague (head of department)
(e) a colleague of your choice (f) more than one colleague?

54. Who do you think should appraise the Headteacher?
(a) adviser (b) choice as for other colleagues
(c) a committee group from the staff (say 2–3 colleagues)
(d) some other group?

55. Should the Headteacher's Review/Appraisal Interview be the   Yes/No/
first each year?   It doesn't
    matter

56. Do you think an agreed written record (appraiser/appraisee) should be:
(a) kept at school (b) sent to the authority (c) both (a) and (b)
(d) not kept at all?

57. In a situation of disagreement on the outcome of an appraisal   Yes/No
process as part of a Staff Development Policy, would you
wish an appeal system to operate?

58. In such an appeal process, would you want a subsequent interview with:
(a) another colleague of your choice (b) an adviser
(c) some other source?
If (c) please specify:

59. Should a review/appraisal interview be voluntary, or in view of the
current climate (and if included in a Staff Development Policy), should
it include all members of staff?
(a) voluntary (b) all staff

60. Would you be happy about an imposed appraisal/   Yes/No
assessment scheme, not part of a Staff Development Policy,
and possibly linked to pay?

61. Would you support the introduction of an appraisal   Yes/No/
process, worked out by staff discussion and part of an   Possibly
overall Staff Development Scheme?

62. In pursuing Staff Development, assuming that maximum and   Yes/No
efficient use is made of existing resources, is it reasonable – if
considered necessary – to expect additional input from the LEA?

63. What sort of help would you be looking for?   Please tick and also
    indicate other
    possible uses for
    financial input.
(a) teacher advisers in school
(b) supply cover to enable visits to other schools
(c) free time to work with other classes of the school
(d) in class support from colleagues on staff
(e) additional equipment
(f) other help:

64. Would you like a system of Mutual Observation introduced?   Yes/No/
   (This means release from your class in order to work closely   Possibly/
   with a colleague. After discussion with your partner you sit   I want to
   in on lessons and observe, taking no active role at all, but   know more
   making notes about your colleague's approach, performance, etc.
   After the lesson you discuss your notes with the view to
   bringing about improved work. The process is then reversed on
   another occasion. This is a very much simplified explanation of a
   scheme that has merits and has been used very successfully
   in some areas.)

65. Are there any other 'Staff Development Practices' you would   Yes/No
   like introduced as part of our policy?
   If 'Yes' please specify:

66. Are there any other areas of education practice/innovation you   Yes/No
   would like us to consider?
   If 'Yes' please specify:

67. Are you prepared to take part in follow-up discussions on   Yes/No
   all aspects of school Staff Development Policy?

Thank you for completing this questionnaire. I have tried to cover as much ground as possible in the questions asked. If you wish to make any other comments that might help in building a Staff Development Policy for our consideration, please add your comments below.

Name:_____

Would you like this Questionnaire returned?   Yes/No

Study F:
The introduction of mutual observation as a central activity in a staff development policy

Background

School F is a three-form entry junior school serving a coastal town in the South East. Its 370 children are organized into twelve classes, three per year group. There is a staffing ratio of Head Teacher plus 13.5 teachers. The school stands on a compact site which it shares with its feeder Infants School.

When I arrived to take up the headship I quickly realized that promotion for key members of staff was not easily achieved – there were few promoted posts available. For my part I pursued a policy of encouraging staff to apply for secondments to extended or postgraduate courses relevant to their needs. This strategy proved successful. Staff gained secondment and returned refreshed and invigorated. In due course I gained secondment and in the course of this, explored the feasibility of introducing mutual observation as a central activity in staff development. This case study outlines the natural history of that initiative and what followed from it.

Accountability, appraisal, assessment and evaluation of teacher performance were receiving a good deal of attention nationally and I had the notion that if activities like mutual observation became a 'norm' within a school it might go some way to meeting the above demands.

Stenhouse (1975) stressed the importance of this type of activity in a teacher's professional development but noted that 'So many seem elated by the discussion of educational ideas, so few are encouraged by close critical scrutiny of their own classrooms'.

The project   The project was introduced to staff in the form of an experiment. Those not involved were close enough to the participants to observe the process and reflect on possibilities. I was reasonably confident that a year group would volunteer their services realizing it could be beneficial to them and to the school in general.

The second-year team of three teachers volunteered to take part. At the first meeting, a model evolved (see Diagram 4) that would operate every Friday morning for six weeks during the Summer Term. It was agreed that each teacher would spend half the morning as an observer then during the second half they themselves would be observed.

The three teachers showed sufficient confidence to engage in the activity, demonstrating the mutual respect each had for the other, but one issue that did cause some concern was 'What was to be observed in the classroom?'. Each teacher suggested that the focus might be their own personal strengths (see diagram). I was concerned that this might 'polarize' the team and suggested that we should delay focusing and initially simply practise being observers. After that we might then select issues that emerged from the early 'field notes'.

Reporting the fieldwork

The pattern agreed for any given observation divided itself into three parts:

1. The classroom observation.
2. Discussion following observer feedback. This was carried out in the lunch hour on the day of the observation by the team of teachers.
3. Agreement on any suggestions regarding the process of observation.

During the first periods of observation there was a predictable reluctance to criticize each other, albeit constructively, or to suggest changes relating to teaching style. Although Mrs Bell raised issues relating to Mrs Delph's classroom practice these were generalized into suggestions that teachers differ in their reaction to classroom organization, groups, noise levels and so on. Mrs Delph referred to Mr Elder's use of a worksheet in a Mathematics lesson. His significant comment was, 'But I rarely work this way', indicating that he had reacted to the presence of an observer by 'playing safe' and preparing a worksheet. This method of working was not seen again in subsequent observation periods.

Mr Elder (observer) focused on Mrs Bell's group activity methods and questioned the amount of time she had given to the Mathematics group compared to other groups. She was very quick to point out that all the groups in turn would receive this new piece of work and it should not be rushed through. Mr Elder responded by congratulating her on her ability to hold 'five' conversations at once in managing her class. That point emphasized the importance of 'humour' prevalent in most of our taped discussions.

Further refinements to the process included a 'grid' sheet for use during observation, and agreement that an 'agenda' should be drawn up prior to the observation by the observed for the observer. These strategies provided a framework in which I could work with the three members of staff concerned. The longer the observations progressed the more the teachers focused their attention on individual children rather than on aspects of their pedagogy.

At the end of the experiment I presented each teacher with this question:

Could you see this process model we developed becoming a 'norm' within a Primary School?

Here are their replies (verbatim).

Mrs Bell

'I think it would be very valuable to adopt this as a regular school practice. I think everyone would have something to gain not only within one year group but observing throughout the school. I think it would be of particular benefit to probationary teachers and to those returning to teaching after a few years' absence. Also, long-standing members of staff may find it refreshing and it may inspire them to try new practices. Mutual observation as a staff development activity may serve to keep us all on our toes and to keep our aims and objectives in sight.

Although the prospect is daunting at first it would become less so if this practice became the norm. I think the practice would bring staff much closer and better able to share problems, ideas etcetera. Personally I would be glad to see the process becoming established but understand that others might find it difficult to participate.'

Mrs Delph

'I certainly found the process valuable. The problems are those of time, disposition of staff and personalities. Time problems can be overcome. Probationers, young inexperienced teachers, older teachers, some of whom may feel insecure when linked with younger teachers "with all the modern ideas" – all these people need to be carefully considered. In insensitive hands, such a project could be destructive. Carefully developed, such a project could provide great strength to a school and its staff. But what are the wider implications of teacher evaluation – to the Education Authorities, to the Governors, to the public...?

I'm not sure about external observers, that's a whole different kettle of fish. On the other hand I wouldn't want to pass a "job or no job" judgement on my own colleagues.'

Mr Elder

'Extremely valuable, but it would have to be introduced very carefully with the more nervous and volatile members of staff in a school. I do think that once the evaluation became run-of-the-mill it is in fact these people who could benefit most – just by seeing that other teachers have bad lessons, children who drive one to distraction and are also unsure of certain aspects of their teaching. Handled correctly and most definitely in an atmosphere of friendly cooperation rather than evaluation *per se*, it could be a real morale booster to a school.'

Headteacher's observations and comments on the process
This process model creates some problems and raises a number of issues for staff:

● Teachers, some more than others, may show anxiety in having an observer in the classroom.

● If colleagues are to become evaluators this must be based on mutual trust and respect.

● A teacher must approach the task in a professional manner and not let pride and personality create a barrier.

● Experienced teachers must not be seen to be 'too clever'. One of the teachers (year leader) was very conscious of this when relating to her younger colleagues.

● Mrs Bell questioned whether an unknown observer would be as sympathetic on her 'bad day' as Mrs Delph had been.

I noted however the following:

● All the teachers questioned more thoroughly what they were doing and why.

● The children did not respond unnaturally to having other teachers in the classroom.

● The observers and observed often referred to observations well after the enquiry was over (that is the value of first-hand experience for teachers).

● Staff were prepared to try new ideas and become self-critical.

● The experiment certainly raised the professional confidence of the teachers concerned. They were pleased to have been part of the process and to some degree became positive gate-keepers in persuading other colleagues of its merit.

Given this experience I was keen to pursue the innovation when I returned from my secondment. Should I suggest to the staff that part of my teaching work-load be used to *make observation possible*? By accident rather than by design a solution emerged – SFSD.

School-focused staff development (SFSD)

The opportunity arose for the school to join a pilot scheme with seven other schools under the auspices of the University of Sussex in conjunction with my Education Authority and the DES.

The purpose of this scheme was for each school to devise a policy for school-based activities that would promote staff development. Each of the pilot schools identified a teacher to be seconded for one term (April–July) who would act as coordinator between the school and the university group. On reflection the choice of that person was crucial. We selected Mr Taylor, a Scale II teacher rather than Head or Deputy Head. In selecting him we were seen to appoint a middle man who could easily communicate with all members of staff as opposed to a senior member of staff with positional authority who might be seen as 'holding the reins' in the decision-making. Mr Taylor's task was to negotiate with staff and reach agreement on activities that would form the basis of an on-going SFSD policy. Mutual Observation was given a high priority.

Activities to be included in the school's staff development policy

1. Teacher files to be established containing information on:
   (a) Job Description
   (b) Courses attended
   (c) Curriculum documents or papers produced by teacher
   (d) Admin. letter relating to teacher
   (e) Notes on Mutual Observation
   (f) Appraisal Statement (one-to-one interview)

2. Counselling
   (a) Career matters
   (b) Interviews (jobs)
       (i) Application
       (ii) Discussion
       (iii) De-briefing
   (c) Experience within school (that is, change of role)

3. Appraisal (or Staff Development Review)

4. Mutual Observation
   (a) Classroom teaching
   (b) Specialist support

5. Induction scheme
   For (a) Probationary staff
       (b) Newly appointed staff
       (c) Supply staff

6. Staff library
   All resources to be fully documented and made available.

7. In-service days
   Programmes to be agreed in advance in conjunction with our SFSD programme.

8. Staff development meetings

9. School guide
   For (a) Staff
       (b) Non-teaching staff
       (c) Supply staff
       (d) Parents etcetera.

Each school in the pilot scheme was given financial resources from the LEA amounting to one supply day per teacher per year. The staff agreed in principle that this resource would be used in the main for Mutual Observation activities.

At our SFSD meetings agreements were reached on where the emphasis for Mutual Observation should be placed. The staff have agreed that any observation sessions will be recorded on a report sheet (see Appendix). The report sheets are then filed under that teacher's name, the Head by agreement having access to all sheets. If any other member of staff wishes access to them then approval must be given by the teacher concerned. By reporting back on the exercise, information can be gleaned by the Head on such matters as:

1. The interaction between the members of staff concerned.
2. The way staff are thinking about an area of concern or curriculum development.
3. Planning future developments: (a) staff needs
   (b) school needs.

We have now reached the stage where observation report sheets are no longer confidential to the teacher, observer and Head, but are referred to at Staff Development meetings. This to some degree still depends on the nature and purpose of the activity.

NB. Whilst observations between staff with agreed agendas was the original aim recent educational initiatives, for instance National Curriculum, have necessitated a shift of focus to whole-staff needs.

Management of mutual observation (within the SFSD policy)

In the early Staff Development meetings it became quite obvious that the weight of opinion was for the Mutual Observation to serve a need, that is Curricular Development, as distinct to developing observation skills *per se*.

Here are two examples from the teacher files to demonstrate this.

Example 1 (Physical Education)
Miss R is a probationary teacher, and as part of her induction she is asked whether any help is required through this activity. Miss R requested to see an experienced teacher, Mrs N (Deputy Head) using the County guidelines (PE) as she felt uncertain about certain aspects, for example:

- terminology;
- how long to allow children to practice;
- how to give the children ideas if they seem short of responses to the tasks set.

The SFSD meeting agreed the number of sessions (4 × 1 hour) to meet this need – the equivalent of one supply teacher for one day.

Miss R and Mrs N agreed the following format:

		Observer	*Observed*
1.	September 26th	Miss R	Mrs N
2.	October 24th	Miss R	Mrs N
3.	November 7th	Mrs N	Miss R
4.	November 14th	Mrs N	Miss R

Comments from Miss R (on Lessons 1 and 2)
During the first two lessons in which I was the observer I particularly noted:

- the getting out and putting away of apparatus;
- Mrs N's experience' of flexibility within the guidelines;
- making the children think and continuing with an activity because the children were involved, as opposed to moving on because the guidelines said so;
- the way children demonstrated to the rest.

Watching Mrs N has helped me in three ways:

1. the pacing of the lesson;
2. general organization of groups and apparatus;
3. the use of guidelines for the basis of the lesson.

Comments from Mrs N (on Lessons 3 and 4)
I became a participant observer once Miss R had got under way. Miss R felt that I would be more useful and less obtrusive!

- I felt Miss R showed considerable courage and professionalism in becoming involved in Mutual Observation in her first term in school.
- Both lessons got off to a good start – used teaching points well.
- Less confidence with the floorwork, which is not surprising. In Lesson 3 particularly the wording of some activities is not always straightforward.
- In her preparation to the lesson she introduced apparatus in an inventive way. The children worked well, striving for a high standard.

Final comment from Miss R
'These sessions have given me a more positive feeling towards the teaching of gymnastics and I feel more confident about what I am doing than I did previously.'

It would seem that this early input into assisting Miss R with her PE lessons had been timely.

Example 2 (Science)
Mr Taylor, who became the SFSD coordinator during the pilot scheme offered his expertise in Science to the staff. The recent development of an SFSD policy enabled him to use the resources of supply cover to gain access to classrooms and offer support. The response of the staff was positive. This was how he proceeded:

Aims
- To demonstrate ideas on classroom organization for practical sessions in a teacher's *own* surroundings with their own class, making it meaningful and applicable.
- To facilitate the possibility of change by introducing practical ideas.
- Provide an experience in classroom observation.

Procedure
- A practical demonstration lesson given by Mr Taylor.
- Class-teacher to observe, make field notes but free to be involved if necessary.
- Following the lesson, discussion to focus on concerns that the class-teacher might have.
- Possibility of further activities/lessons would be considered in the light of discussions.

Observation lessons
Mr Taylor managed to cover eleven classrooms with a wide range of scientific topics and varied responses.

Immediate comments following the exercise
1. The observed (that is, Science specialist) gained by having to concentrate his thoughts to the structure and content of the lesson as well as the presentation of it – a practice we sometimes inevitably slip out of in our own classroom.

2. The observer (class-teacher) gained by experiencing another teacher at work which leads to self-questioning. The pooling of ideas is valuable, the observer had to look critically at the lesson and expound on it.

3. There was a wide variety of experience in observational skills amongst the staff. Experience in observation is essential for fully effective sessions.

4. Teachers differed in their aptitude to acquire observational skills. This needs careful induction and preparation.

5. It is essential that the ground rules have been negotiated prior to the exercise.

6. It is necessary to make notes during the observation. These notes can then be referred to in discussion.

Citing these two examples demonstrates the positive approach shown by the teachers, thus making the management initiative relatively straightforward. The staff had agreed the importance of induction for new staff, hence Miss R's built-in opportunity to use Mutual Observation as a means of improving her skills in physical education.

There have been occasions when large groups of teachers have met on an in-service day to discuss areas of curriculum but without follow up. Those days can prove to be ineffective.

The early attempt of Mr Taylor in his science initiative, by making use of policy agreements, allowed the theory and discussion of such a day to be put into practice within the setting of one's own school. As Head, my management task has been that of pacing and organizing the exercise together with offering support with resources as the need arose. I also played a pastoral role when either the observer or observed needed assurance or advice.

Recently we introduced a new Mathematics scheme throughout the school in one fell swoop. Many Headteachers (managers) would have been pleased to have successfully implemented the change itself, especially if consensus agreement had been reached amongst the staff. Through our SFSD policy we were able to take this major innovation one step further. Through our SFSD meetings we agreed to focus all our Mutual Observation sessions for one year on the implementation of this scheme. This gave *all* members of staff the opportunity of comparing and contrasting ideas across the year group.

This exercise greatly enhanced a team approach to development. The staff saw the value of the sharing of ideas and problems in the meetings that followed. The scheme suggested many practical group-work ideas to assist children in their understanding of mathematical concepts. Those members of staff who may have limited the introduction of practical group work had the opportunity to see the scheme in action in other classrooms, thus enriching their own performance of practical ideas.

Quite often an innovation in itself can create enough energy to see it through the early stages, but once it's up and running what next? Mutual Observation can be used as a central strategy to keep the development under surveillance and to act as an effective means of review from time to time depending on need.

Teachers are often described as 'doing' people and have been known to react negatively to theory and discussion especially if they feel it to be too removed from the shop-floor – their actual job. Mutual Observation bridges that gap. It puts the teacher in a learning situation that is as near as it can be to their real situation.

A word of warning. It is very important for the ground work to be thoroughly dealt with *before* a policy incorporating an activity like Mutual Observation is introduced.

The staff always felt that sufficient consultation had taken place and that they had been party to the decision-making. Trust was paramount.

Eraut (1978) asks two questions of teachers; firstly, why do teachers change or fail to change, and secondly, how do teachers learn? Mutual observation allows teachers to participate in a learning situation that is based on trust and seeks to generate rigour. Both are necessary ingredients in the process of effective change.

References

ERAUT, M. (1978). 'Accountability at School Level – some Options'. In: BECKER, T. and MACLURE, S. (Eds). *Accountability in Education*. Slough: NFER.

STENHOUSE, L. (1975). *An Introduction to Curriculum Research and Development*. London: Heinemann.

Comment

The initiative outlined in Study F indicates just how much time it takes for a change to take place. Negotiation was the major strategy adopted by the Head who was undertaking a piece of action-research rather than seeking to push through an innovation. The starting point was experimental. Staff involved were allowed to agree *their* agendas, devise their methods of observation and in so doing came to see the value of the change. The sequence of management is characterized by the identification of needs, consultation, negotiation and involvement of staff in decision-making. The Headteacher's stance was to facilitate change. One indicator of the success of the innovation is the fact that staff no longer feel that observation reports should remain confidential. In using mutual observation to promote the monitoring of teaching and learning under open reporting the Head is more able to link two key aspects of the development process:

1. The needs of individual members of staff.
2. The development of whole-school initiatives founded on observations made in relation to 1.

A further noticeable strategy was to promote the initiative through the leadership of a Scale 2 teacher rather than by means of a senior member of staff. It is evident that the Head is able to adapt his style to meet the requirements of a changing situation.

Questions for the reader's consideration

- The Headteacher indicates that the evaluation of the effectiveness of mutual classroom observation is not easy to achieve. What criteria would you consider appropriate to use?

- In what ways could this school build on the process of mutual observation when making changes in relation to the National Curriculum?

Study F: Report Sheet, Mutual Observation

Observer: _____   *Date of observation:* _____

Observed: _____

Brief outline of aspects to be observed:
(put reasons if you think it useful)

Duration of observation:
This session and its reciprocal one was/was not linked to previous ones.
This session and its reciprocal one will/will not be linked to future ones.

_____

Diagram 4:
MUTUAL OBSERVATION MODEL

Initial meeting : Friday 18th May, 3.30pm – 5.00pm

Purpose: to agree the model

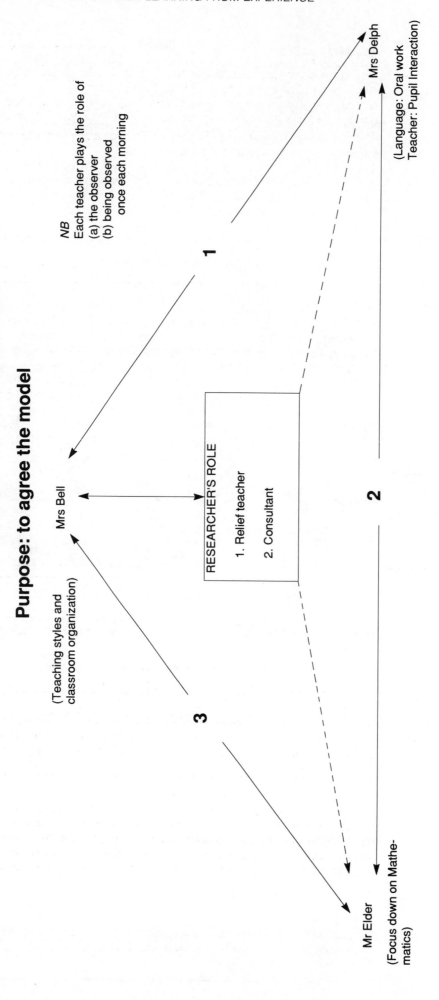

NB
Each teacher plays the role of
(a) the observer
(b) being observed
once each morning

Mrs Delph

(Language: Oral work
Teacher: Pupil Interaction)

1

Mrs Bell

RESEARCHER'S ROLE

1. Relief teacher

2. Consultant

(Teaching styles and
classroom organization)

2

3

Mr Elder

(Focus down on Mathe-
matics)

NB *The triangle of teachers is ideal: if the order
is reversed then they all see one another as
(a) observers or (b) being observed*

Report

Notes: The headings are for guidance only. Use continuation sheets as necessary. Ignore headings and make report on a separate sheet if desired.

A copy *must* go into the file of both Observer and Observed, as a record of the session. However, additional, confidential reports may be retained by participants only. It is expected that this report is completed by both participants together.

Comments of the observer (*not advice* – just observations)

Comments of the observed (avoid defensive statements)

Changes in teaching/classroom activities proposed as a result of observation.
NB: *not* recommended changes

Observer:

Observed:

Area of any future observation: _____

Contents to be disclosed to no one other than Observer and Observed without the permission of both.

Study G: The Curriculum Newsletter – a catalyst for action

Background

School G is an 8 to 12 Middle School housed in the 1961 building of an ex secondary school. The school opened in 1971 with 360 pupils, grew to 730 on roll by 1979 followed by rapid contraction until 1986 when the roll stood at 260 pupils. It is likely to stabilize at a roll of 400 pupils.

Organizations are always changing. A critical factor in organizational effectiveness is the ability to respond quickly and successfully as new issues appear on the educational agenda. Schools in particular continuously experience the turbulence of change. Parents, teachers, governors, local authorities and central government have different perceptions as to how to improve the quality of education children receive. In being responsive to these pressures schools need to balance their concerns for people with an equal commitment to accomplishing agreed aims and tasks through purposeful teaching.

The central task of schools is to promote and support the quality of pupils' learning experiences within an agreed curriculum which is sensitive to individual needs. This mission statement will be implemented within the context of the educational philosophy of the school. Headteachers and their staff will be instrumental in developing such a philosophy. However, if its translation into practice is to be achieved successfully, it must be shared, developed and moderated by a genuine dialogue with all the partners in the educational contract. This dialogue will need to be part of a continuous process with the emerging policies subject to systematic review.

The consideration of four questions is vital in order to start this developmental process:

- Where have we come from? (a cultural and historical perspective).
- Where are we now? (review and analysis of current position).
- Where do we want to get to? (a vision of the future).
- How are we going to get there? (process and action plan).

Where have we come from?

School G is a coeducational day school for pupils in the age range of eight to twelve years of age. The fluctuating school roll has been indicated at the beginning of this study. The former headteacher of the secondary school and many of his staff formed the establishment of 16 teachers in 1971. Between 1971 and 1979 a further 18 members of staff were appointed. A new headteacher was appointed just after the school started to contract in 1980. The school has currently 11 full-time staff (with some part-time support) who now work as traditional class-teachers and a Deputy Head. Many staff have experienced major changes in their roles from working as subject specialists to becoming broadly-based teachers working across the curriculum in a classroom environment, educating children through the process of firsthand experience. These changes have been achieved by developing our own in-service training programmes within a year team structure. The school has a growing reputation, particularly in Science and Computing, Environmental Studies, Drama and Media work. The parents are very supportive and have a successful association which actively participates in the life of the school.

Where are we now?

The new initiatives we are taking in the school at present are part of a process that started two years ago as a consequence of the concerns many staff had been expressing. The school had experienced three to four years of industrial action and as a consequence the curriculum was showing signs of stagnation. Forward planning had become particularly problematic and the communications network between parents and staff was under significant strain. The numbers on roll were continuing to decline. One consequence of the Education Act and the introduction of 'parental choice' was for the school to become less competitive with other schools. Fewer pupils implied less staff and a potential distortion of the curriculum we could offer parents and their children. Clearly these trends needed to be reversed quickly. The senior management team started to look to the future and began to anticipate the potential influence of a National Curriculum on the school. The development of the LEA's Primary School review procedures with the Governors, the possible introduction of schemes of appraisal and changes in In-service Training of Teachers (INSET) funding all influenced the climate within this team.

Curriculum review and school esteem
Two initial decisions were taken as a result of staff discussions. Firstly, to conduct our own curriculum review of each area of the curriculum as part of a planned development opportunity for the Deputy Head. His brief was to work with other colleagues in each curriculum area in order to establish school policy for the next two years. This task included the identification of the knowledge, concepts, skills and attitude to be taught, the resources to be used in support of this work, recommendations as to methods of evaluation to be used with appropriate record keeping systems, aspects of the curriculum worthy of inclusion or given increased attention in addition to items requiring less attention or removal from the programme. Thus we would be able to establish our future priorities and match them into our school development plan for the next two years. Secondly we would enter a submission for the 'schools curriculum development award scheme' in order to build on those aspects of our community life which had been successful over many years, start to work on improving the quality of education provided for the children and rediscover our strengths and self-esteem.

The further articulation of these concerns and issues were helped by the headteacher being involved in 'OTTO' training programmes at the University of Sussex. The aim of all these activities was to generate a shared sense of purpose and a vision for the future to which we would all become committed and determined to achieve.

here do we want to get to?

The notion being articulated here is that the goals of education should be clearly stated in order to assist in the clarification of key tasks. Such goals and explicitly stated outcomes assist the process of evaluation. They act as reference points when talk turns to the quality of provision.

The vision embraces the view that children should enjoy coming to school and show a lively interest in the challenges presented to them by teachers. That pupils should learn from first hand experience and acquire a broad array of knowledge, skills, concepts and attitudes which should be explicitly stated and shared with parents and other members of the community so that they can be actively engaged in the educational process. The development of this partnership is vital to the success of the enterprise and the achievements of the stated educational outcomes.

But having such a vision is not sufficient; it needs the commitment of others. There is also a need to ensure that it shapes the policies, plans and daily activities of the organization and that the values, feelings and beliefs it represents are shared.

How are we going to get there?

The curriculum award submission created much interest with pupils, staff and parents but did not in itself present significant growth points. Similarly the curriculum review, although producing a series of priorities and courses of action, did not capture the imagination of everybody. However it did reveal many deep seated anxieties of colleagues which revolved around the issues of the relationship between teacher and taught, the freedom to take independent action within an agreed framework and the accompanying concepts related to the professional autonomy of the classroom teacher. Although the debate was lively no significant progress was made. The need for a tangible objective and plan of action was paramount. The interests of parents did not figure highly at that time. The catalyst came from quite a different route.

A colleague's son had recently changed schools, and in a quiet moment he asked the naive question, 'What are you going to do at school tomorrow?' The answer was immediate, 'Well in Subject A we are going to do this tomorrow, and that the next day etcetera, it's great. But in Subject B we sometimes don't even know half-way through the lesson.' The parental perspective to our dilemma became clearer. Did many parents ask those same questions? Was it not the case that many wished to support their child's education? At the next Parents Association meeting the story was shared with them and the response was equally immediate. They were genuinely interested and furthermore they sometimes felt resentful at being excluded from knowing what their children did at school. Similarly the story was shared with staff and those with children confirmed that as parents they readily identified with the thoughts and feelings expressed, and had not seriously considered translating these concerns into their own professional life. What constituted appropriate action? How would we communicate this information to parents? Would parents be content to have a non-interventionist role? Did we as teachers have the professional confidence to enter into this risky dialogue? What would we do if we lost control of the situation? How much extra work would we have to do? These were some of the most persistent questions to be asked by colleagues. Clearly there were many anxieties to be alleviated.

The view developed that we did have the confidence because we knew we were doing a good job of work that would stand up to public examination. The limited evidence suggested that parents would welcome such an initiative from the school and that in the current climate there were positive advantages to working more closely with them. We were going to develop a different style of partnership from which we would all benefit. Our Chairman of Governors saw it as a very positive step forward and commented that if our presentation was on target our numbers on roll would rise very quickly, and therefore any extra work we did would be well rewarded.

The majority of colleagues were feeling more at ease. The idea was developed on two principles: 1. We will make mistakes so let's make them quickly and learn from them quickly; so we must listen carefully to the 'customers' for feedback. 2. Let's do our best to get it right first time, so that we will all have had a successful experience.

Tactical options

Three approaches were considered:

1. **Parents' meetings.** These were to be called by classteachers who would explain the programme for the next term. A briefing meeting would be held, followed by the children engaging in the task, followed by a parents' evening to share the outcomes. Not everybody was confident about how to undertake such a programme of work, and others felt it was going too far too quickly. This option was rejected.

2. **Publication of concise curriculum documents.** This received a similar response. A good idea but not enough time and too much hard work. This also was rejected.

3. **The publication of a letter to parents outlining the term's programme.** This received the most favourable response although many colleagues did not feel confident enough in their knowledge across the curriculum to write such a letter. However, they were prepared to work together and produce a 'Curriculum Newsletter' from each year-group team provided the time-scale for its introduction was not unreasonable and took into account the current workload.

Tactical choice and 'action plan'

The outcome of the discussions with all the staff was that the 'Curriculum Newsletter' had become self-selecting. The agreement reached at the beginning of the Spring Term was that the letters would be phased in over the next two terms, year group by year group, and that all four teams would be in a position to publish their own letters at the start of the next academic year. Three letters would be written during that year with the success of the enterprise being reviewed in the Summer Term. The first-year team were keen to publish their letter after the current Spring Half-Term and pioneer the process. Their particular interest was that this was the major term for potential new parents to choose schools for September and that such a publication would give us a competitive advantage over other schools. Some colleagues believed this to be a highly risky strategy. In order to alleviate these not unreasonable fears a 'dry run' was planned. One class-teacher in the first year invited the parents to school and briefed them on the initiative. The parents were enthusiastic and made many constructive comments on the content of the letter. One problem that emerged from this dialogue was the lack of a working definition of the curriculum that parents could understand, in addition to their traditional concerns about the teaching of Mathematics, spelling and homework.

In anticipation of the National Curriculum it was agreed to use the core and foundation subjects we expected the Act to contain and to identify areas of study where subject integration was planned.

The Curriculum Newsletter contained a brief description of the tasks children would be following in each of these areas. 'Hot and Cold' was the title of the integrated work for the term and the notes about Science, History, Geography, Social Studies, Religious Education and the Creative Arts reflected this theme. Television programmes and books children would find useful were identified as were the educational visits for the term, so that parents could plan their support where appropriate. Language work, Mathematics and Physical Education were given separate paragraphs. An outline of the way children were being taught Mathematics was included, together with practical advice for parents who wished to help children to improve their spelling. A clear statement of school policy concerning homework was given. Parents were encouraged to participate fully in the programme and to use the school's homework diaries as a means of communicating their interests or concerns with class-teachers in addition to normal appointments or classroom visits. The first letter was published after Spring Half-Term. Copies were given to all potential parents for the following September intake of pupils. An example of a first-year curriculum newsletter is provided at the end of this study.

Initial review of progress

The impact of the initiative was closely monitored by feedback from colleagues, members of the Parents Association committee and school governors. This process culminated in a very successful series of individual parent–teacher interviews at our normal Open Evenings at the end of the Spring Term. Although these have always been constructive and pleasant many parents observed how much easier it was for them to talk about their children's work and progress without the fear of being labelled an interfering or complaining parent. Members of the teaching staff supported these observations and commented on the positive nature of parental attitudes even when pupils were not making the expected progress each partner desired.

The most rewarding outcome of the experience was that all the year-group teams advanced their plans and decided to publish their own letters at the start of the Summer Term rather than waiting until September. Some colleagues expressed the view that they felt under pressure to publish, but such concerns were diminished when the effect on our admission numbers for September were confirmed. Although other factors were present in the equation, for example a first-year tam with a good public reputation and a slight increase in our feeder schools population, the significance of moving from being under-subscribed by 30 pupils in the current year to exceeding the admission number of 90 by a further six children was not lost on anybody.

Developmental concerns

The Curriculum Newsletter had given the school a powerful tool for forward planning, a commitment by colleagues to an agreed programme of work and a means of reviewing termly progress. But would it be reflected in the curriculum-in-action and appropriate record-keeping systems? Were the implications compatible with the new teachers' conditions of service and time budgeting to be imposed on colleagues in September?

Everybody wanted to see the agreed programme translated into classroom practice. Individual subject coordinators wanted an appropriate allocation of time to be given to their special interest by all members of staff. A four-week project was undertaken as curriculum letters were being written to establish our current curriculum balance. Each member of staff was asked to record in broad terms the time they actually allocated to each curriculum area. The evidence from each year group was compared with the guidelines published by the Local Education Authority, as a consequence of a recent survey and information being suggested by the Department of Education and Science. The results clearly indicated that we were spending significantly more time on teaching Mathematics and English than recommended and, equally, insufficient time on the Humanities, Science and the Creative Arts.

After a lively discussion in the Summer Term, a response to these findings was built into the next year's timetable. Although it is too early to make a considered judgement, the evidence from the end-year curriculum review suggests that there has been no drop in standards as some colleagues had predicted. Children appear to be enjoying Mathematics and English more than a year ago. The amount of repetitive work has been reduced significantly and progress tests indicate an upward trend in scores. Most class-teachers' judgements support these preliminary results. However the frustrations generated by time pressure have not disappeared but have only reappeared in a different form.

The issues concerned with record keeping were resolved by year teams planning and reviewing the term's work using the Curriculum Newsletter as framework for professional discussion, and within that context individual class-teachers conducted a more detailed forecast of work to be undertaken by their children. Progress achieved or problems encountered every half-term would be noted. This was an improvement on the previous rather haphazard system of record keeping. The successful keeping of individual pupil curriculum records and personal profiles on children continued to be the responsibilities of class-teachers.

The school emerged out of these muddy waters of change in the autumn with an agreed programme of work, more effective forward planning, improved record-keeping procedures, a more balanced curriculum and a system of curriculum review. Communications between parents and school have greatly improved as has the professional dialogue between colleagues, and the school is oversubscribed.

The catalyst to all this development has been the publication of a 'Curriculum Newsletter' (see page 50) for parents making more explicit the work of the school.

The future

Each of the year group teams has successfully published four curriculum newsletters. Parental feedback has been positive, and many of them have been able to take part in the daily life of the school. The newsletter has also helped working partners to support their children at home and not to feel excluded from the process. A different style of partnership is being slowly developed where parental interests and concerns are perceived as being legitimate and constructive, and not as a threat or a take-over bid. Mutual trust is a hard earned and fragile entity and we will all need to work continuously every year to consolidate this relationship.

The school curriculum is now more broadly based and balanced than in former years. Progression and continuity still present difficulties, particularly in the Humanities and Creative Arts and sometimes between year group. We also need to review, in this context, cross phase relationships with other schools in our local network. More fundamentally we need to continually ask the questions, 'Is everything we teach worthwhile and relevant to children?' and 'Are the learning experiences we offer children successfully matched to their abilities and needs?

Recently the concept of the newsletter has been called into question. After four editions a variety of items appear regularly in the text. Colleagues are now asking, 'Is there another way of communicating this information to parents without the repetition which is beginning to appear?' One solution being canvassed by two year teams is the production of a guide for parents which explicitly states the objectives most children will achieve by the time they transfer to secondary school, particularly in Mathematics, English and Science where the repetition is currently occurring. The debate is only just beginning, but again the newsletter is acting as a catalyst by moving us into the next phase of the vision for the future. If we are able to define these educational outcomes explicitly then we may have more effective tools to answer questions concerning curriculum progression and continuity, relevance and match for individual children. We would also have the means of establishing appropriate criteria for evaluating the curriculum. The school development plan for next year starts to address these issues with special reference to language development and the Humanities.

We have made a successful start but all the available evidence suggests an exciting and challenging future.

School G: Curriculum Newsletter

September, 1988

Dear Parents,

The long-awaited September entry date has come and gone. Your children are now pupils at _____ Middle School and we have an exciting programme of study and events for them in this, their first term.

Below is an outline of the work we hope to explore. With this information you will be in a position to support and encourage your children so that they may achieve their personal best. We hope that you will work with us to establish good practice in work both at school and at home, a high standard of personal organization and frequent opportunities for sharing books with your child – the child reading to you, you reading to your children.

Language (English) is the basis of everything we do. We teach English across every curriculum area. Language and *literature* may arise from science, from Environmental Studies, from Geography, History, etc. Alongside this we encourage children to develop their interest in, and their enjoyment of, our own literary heritage of stories and poems.

We hope that by the end of their 1st year every child will be writing in joined up handwriting and in ink, so the *practice* of *handwriting* is a classroom exercise. We also hope that by then all children will be able to construct simple sentences, will have improved their standard of reading and increased their vocabulary – a giant step towards this will be taken in their Autumn term.

Spelling will be learnt from the subjects taught, from the children's own writing and through the Blackwell Spelling Workshop. When helping your child to spell we suggest you use the method

LOOK   COVER   WRITE   CHECK

This encourages the children to be responsible for their own learning. They do not need to be 'asked' spellings.

Spoken English is as important as written work and we give considerable time to this.

Across all subject areas children will be learning simple study skills.

This term we have a central theme. In its broadest terms this is 'Space'. We shall start where the child is with the immediate space around of school, village, area, and widen his understanding as we move into the realms of outer space.

Science will take place in the lab., in the classroom and outside. The lab. will provide scope for 12 investigations related to space – plants, the turning earth, air, the earth's pull, night and day. Television may be used as a classroom stimulus as will direct observation of the world around us.

In *Mathematics* the children will work at their own rate within the Primary Mathematics Scheme. It is easy for you to be aware of what they are doing from the grid on the front of their workbook. If they are doing a section on measurement you could add interest at home with baking and weighing. The scheme is based on practical experience, with the children working systematically through a workbook, wordcards and a textbook. It is not a 'race'. Children are encouraged to see the importance of learning from their mistakes. It is these that tell us the weak areas and are therefore very important in learning.

Time for *oral mathematics* is given in class (tables, number bonds, e.g. $7 + ? = 10$; $17 + ? = 20$; mathematical language – product, difference, total). Once again you can help with this at home.

Physical Education. Every class will have an hour's PE lesson where the children's use of space will be explored through agility. Apparatus will be introduced. In addition to this will be an hour's games session. Ball skills of varying types will be taught and there will be opportunities for varying sports.

Music. Every class will have 1½ hours of music a week. One session will be with our music specialist. The children will learn to read and make music, to sing and to appreciate music of the composers. There may be some lessons in eurhythmics.

Environmental Studies/History/Geography
The above three subjects are generally known to the children as project work or discovery studies. They will develop from our central theme and from a television stimulus. They will sometimes be historical, sometimes geographical and sometimes environmental. Trips out of school will increase the children's learning. Areas covered will include the history of the house system at Heathside, the significance of the school's name, awareness of the immediate surroundings of the school and its neighbouring villages, dairy farming in Heathside, Shire's position in GB, the elderly in our community and space exploration.

Religious Education. Here we are concerned with the children's moral education – caring for each other and the community. We hope to teach them an understanding of the terms Bible, Old Testament, New Testament, BC and AD and something of the meaning of Christmas and the events leading up to it.

Art/Craft/Computer Studies/Home Economics
One afternoon a week will be an Activity Session of 1½ hours. Children will have scope for needlework, cookery, pottery, art and craft, woodwork, computer skills, drama and problem-solving through Craft, Design and Technology. Each activity will be studied for a few weeks in a rotating system of social groupings across the 1st and 2nd years.

Over and above this will be opportunities for the above activities in the child's own class.

Social Development. It has been a tradition at Heathside to have a Lower School Christmas Production. This provides great scope for group awareness, self-discipline, listening skills and enjoyment. All 1st and 2nd year children take part and in so doing increase their own personal development and maturity. This year's production is entitled 'Christmas Capers' and was first performed at Heathside in 1980.

Homework Policy. All children in the year group have a small homework notebook. This is designed for 2 way communication. The children will bring home a note of what they have to do and thus you will be able to monitor their work. Should you wish to comment on some aspect of the homework (e.g. a child's difficulty, or the very rare event of a child not being able to do the work because of a domestic problem) then you can do so in the notebook.

At this stage we expect the children to work for about 25–30 minutes per evening. This may be reviewed throughout the year. *All* children will have homework. It may take the form of follow-up work from class or it may be learning, reading, researching or writing. Please talk with your children about their work.

With this information you are in a position to help your children do their best. We shall be most appreciative of your help both in the classroom and out, and do hope that if you have not already been screened by Shire you will seriously apply to us for one of the Shire forms for parents working with children.

Should you be planning any family visits to London this term and would like to consider visiting places connected with our topic I should suggest The London Planetarium, Marylebone Road, and The Geological Museum, Exhibition Road.

Plastic Bags. We have found that a large zipped plastic bag is very useful to the children for carrying maths workbooks, homework, letters, etc. to and from school. These can be purchased from me at 35p per bag.

Yours sincerely,

1st Year Co-ordinator.

Comment

A great deal of explanatory power is placed on the part played by the curriculum newsletter in clarifying and boosting the sense of purpose experienced by staff. The process appears to have acted somewhat in the fashion of a magnifying glass, causing staff to raise questions in relation to the curriculum, its balance, and current procedures in assessing pupils and recording their progress. The strategy was not without risk, but to date no parent appears to have violated existing norms of teacher–parent relationships. In aiming to raise parents' knowledge of what happens in school the strategy appears to have raised the level of staff awareness on a number of central issues. This augurs well though it is likely that such effects were not anticipated at the outset. It would seem important for the Head to monitor the curriculum-in-action in order to establish the degree of match between the espoused curriculum of the newsletter with the curriculum-in-action of individual classrooms. The active involvement of staff has been accomplished. The postscript indicates that home support is beginning to take place and parental involvement in the school's daily life has increased. Evaluation now seems essential in order to establish the range of practice the initiative has precipitated.

Questions for the reader's consideration

- What aspects of school–parent relationships do you think School G should now begin to develop? Why?

- What measures do you think might be taken to avoid repetition and routine creeping in to the newsletter strategy?

- In what ways would you expect a curriculum newsletter for first-year pupils to differ from one relating to fourth-year pupils? Why?

Study H: Planned Developmental Opportunities – a strategy for growth

Background
School H is a combined First and Middle School serving a small village and army camp on the outskirts of a rapidly developing town. There are 110 pupils organized into six classes, one for each year from 5 to 9 and two for the 9 to 12 age groups.

I first encountered the notion of a Planned Developmental Opportunity during a One Term Training Opportunity (OTTO) programme, when the relationships between Headteachers and Deputy Headteachers were explored in terms of partnership and mentorship rather than separate roles within a school. The PDO was aimed to develop particular managerial skills within a supportive framework. The practicalities of such opportunities were not foreign to my own philosophy of enabling teachers to develop their skills in pursuit of professional goals and promotion aspirations. Such projects however were haphazard and, like Topsy, just seemed to grow with no analysis on my part as to their effectiveness in managerial terms. I was aware nevertheless that they appeared to lead to the promotion of successive Deputies to Headship.

The removal of a prefabricated classroom provided the opportunity to create an Environmental Study area. My Deputy was keen to develop such a project and my secondment for a term enabled her to develop the first stage of the initiative in her own way during her period of acting headship. My role was to be that of consultant to the process. All the key elements of task management were there to be explored.

Interpersonal skills – communication

Having made her plans her first objective was to gain the support of the staff, which would be crucial to success. This was tackled at her first staff meeting, when she described how she envisaged the area could be used as an outdoor classroom for the whole school to use, and suggested various features which could be incorporated and invited their suggestions and participation. The idea was well received and so she proceeded to outline the anticipated problems and how she proposed to deal with them. These were mainly related to the provision of manpower for the physical work of making a pond and landscaping the area, and financing the project. Motivating the staff presented no problems initially – it was as the project dragged on beyond the planned time-scale that enthusiasm diminished and needed to be revived; a much more difficult task.

Resources

It was now necessary to involve other agencies. Planning permission from County Hall was already being processed and proved to be a frustrating delaying factor. The school's Governing Body, Ground Maintenance officers at both County Hall and Area Education Office and the Inspectorate were approached for practical advice – all were cooperative and supported the deputy in her next appeal for parental support. The latter was a continuing disappointment with only minimal response, however there were sufficient helpers to make a start when planning permission finally came.

Finance

The intended prime beneficiaries inspiring the project were of course the children, and their early involvement was important. Their contributions were in the form of submitting designs for the layout, and in planning fund raising. Several events were organized during the term and were well supported by most of the staff and children. Raising money proved to be much easier than had been anticipated but most of the organization fell on the Acting Head – delegation to the Acting Deputy was not very successful and she depended on the goodwill of others on the staff. Delegation involved managerial skills that were not sufficiently developed at that stage and awareness of the problem came at a later review.

Problem-solving

Projects rarely proceed without problems to be solved. Several manifested themselves, some related to physical difficulties in preparing the ground, others were due to human bureaucratic errors, others to availability of resources – all led to delays and required regular reviews and redefinition of priorities in short- and long-term time plans. These inevitably affected the enthusiasm of all involved including the Deputy who came to realize that tenacity towards goal achievement was an essential leadership quality and difficult to maintain – projects cannot be abandoned lightly when many others are involved.

The management of change

The project took far longer than expected, and in that time situations and attitudes changed. Other curricular initiatives had to be developed, supportive parents left and new ones were recruited. The status of the Deputy changed from Acting Head back to Deputy and later this position was handed over to someone else during a prolonged absence. Delegating the project to someone who was not the initiator brought it to a virtual standstill – ownership of the task was crucial to its success.

For delegation to be real it should be real in its consequences, and I saw my role as a supportive one. I avoided intervention other than in situations that could only be dealt with at Headteacher level, for instance in initiating planning permission and calling in external agencies to solve apparently intractable problems on the site. During my one-term secondment I was supplied with information on current progress and on my return the control of the process was delegated to the Deputy. There was only one point where I intervened. This was when external contractors were called in and the Deputy became dependent on them to complete their task. They in their turn blamed external constraints as the reasons for failure to meet their commitments, a factor which caused considerable frustration.

Learning points

When the project had been completed there was a final review and the Deputy identified several areas where she had gained insights into her own performance as a leader. There was recognition of the need for rigorous monitoring to ensure that agreed action did take place. It was also recognized that leadership may require one to challenge the decisions of others. She acknowledged the difficulty of maintaining motivation in others, of the need to adopt a variety of styles to suit different situations and audiences. Above all it built her self-confidence so that she could tackle larger projects in a more informed way.

Overview

If teachers are to experience professional growth, opportunities to practice a variety of managerial skills should be made available within controlled conditions. These can be changed as competency increases. Headteachers will need to exercise judgement as to the appropriate level and type of activity to suit the individual, within the constraints of the particular post held in the school. Delegation of authority requires preparation via a mutually agreed plan in which opportunities to seek advice are clearly stated. Pacing of the activity needs careful consideration – too much too soon might prove stressful for particular individuals. It requires mutual trust between the participants and this implies honesty for constructive criticism at analytical stages.

Headteachers may find it difficult to delegate to a member of the team, perceiving it as a diminution of their authority. This is particularly true if the Deputy is seen as a subordinate. If, however, the Deputy is viewed as a genuine partner in the management of the school a climate conducive to planned developmental opportunities can be created and in the words of our OTTO tutor – 'provide an experience to take away into Headship'.

Comment

The concept of planned developmental opportunities arose out of work with Deputy Heads and is based on a particular stance towards learning. It is predicated on the Rogerian notion that no one ever teaches anything to anyone else, since all learning is essentially an act of self-appropriation. What the leader does is to construct opportunities for professional development having first considered threshold levels of knowledge, understanding and experience that are likely to be called into play in the achievement of the goal. In this case study the Headteacher stood by the judgements the Deputy Head had made on occasions when it would have been much easier to step in and take over. Some Heads may find this difficult since their orientation towards task completion takes precedence over their concern for learning. That is not to say that learners should be left to themselves. That would be abdication rather than delegation. Delegation is made more effective if targets are set and feedback points established from the outset. Debriefing the person on completion of the goal is an essential characteristic of the PDO process, since it is here that the kinds of skill, knowledge and insight acquired are mutually explored.

Experience alone is insufficient to ensure significant learning. Critical reflection on the experiences undergone, the abstraction of key ideas that lie at the centre of the experience(s) and the capacity to draw upon these during active exploration of alternative courses of action are important factors which heighten the learning process.

The concept of planned development opportunities is a useful one for Headteachers to consider for there are many such learning opportunities created by the requirements of the Education Reform Act. Conceptualizing goals and tasks in terms of skills, understandings and competences makes it much more enriching than simply giving individuals jobs to do. Constructing such opportunities requires skill but there is no reason why they should not be mutually constructed by Head and delegatee. When a task is completed or a goal achieved the effective manager asks not 'How well did you do?' or 'How did it go?', but 'What did you learn?' – a question which initiates the process of critical reflection. It also provides opportunities to consider the management sequences appropriate to the goal at hand.

Questions for the reader's consideration

- How might you construct a development opportunity for (a) a probationer on your staff and (b) for an experienced member of staff whom you consider to be somewhat demotivated?

- How do Headteachers engage in developmental opportunities? – who might act in the role of mentor?

Commentary on case studies E to H

Development policies and programmes

Each of the studies in this section is concerned with the professional development of staff, the sustaining of professional commitment and the fostering of development at the level of the individual *and* the school as a whole. The studies reveal how four Headteachers went about that process. In two of the schools (E and F) considerable time had been spent on formulating, and constructing with staff, written policies on staff development. That process itself *is* staff development in action. Both Heads acknowledge the benefits which such a policy has brought to their schools: renewed commitment; a clearer sense of direction; a more useful staffing structure; better appreciation of roles; acknowledgement of the need to monitor.

Not all teachers achieve promotion, nor do all of them seek it. Some seek it and fail to gain preferment. But all teachers have careers and some will spend considerable periods of time in the same school. It is important for heads to recognize the features of a career within a school and effective Headteachers will ensure that they pay attention to the particular needs of such staff. Staff development policies remind us of this need. Policy only exists when it is implemented and written documents themselves may achieve little. It is therefore important to note the value of having current programmes of action within the policy which keep it alive. Schools E and F keep their policies energized in that way.

The precise features of a staff development policy and the characteristics of developmental programmes will be unique to each school. In Study E curriculum and organizational tasks were renegotiated to produce an organizational structure which staff played a significant part in creating. One outcome of increased involvement by staff in the running of the school was to raise awareness of the skills and abilities possessed by colleagues. This is an interesting point. Unless special arrangements are made, the core act of teaching frequently takes place in private within the four walls of a classroom. Once teachers have been provided with *arenas for action* it becomes possible for them to establish new identities which, as in Study E, may have consequences for them in terms of promotion. That is of course a happy outcome and quickly earns a school a reputation on the local grapevine, but a major criterion in the evaluation of staff development programmes will be the degree to which they have resulted in improvements at the classroom level and increased the sense of shared purpose.

Staff reviews

Staff reviews played a significant role in the development programme of Study E and the Head was prepared to demonstrate his commitment to their value by submitting himself to a review interview involving an LEA adviser and two members of his staff. Such interviews are labour intensive and the Head quite properly questions their feasibility without the input of additional resources – a point endorsed by each of the pilot projects in Teacher Appraisal. As the process of review interviews becomes commonplace, it will require increasing sensitivity and skill on the part of the Head to sustain commitment and avoid the dangers of monotony.

Staff review interviews provide the opportunity to evaluate past performance and negotiate mutually agreed targets for individual development. The Headteacher or Deputy has sufficient knowledge of each member of staff and the context in which they work to engage constructively in the process. Review interviews for Headteachers are far more problematic. It is not a question of manpower alone. The interviewer(s) need to have sufficient inside knowledge to enable them to place the evidence and information supplied by the Headteacher in context. Contextual knowledge is also required if they are to help in negotiating meaningful and achievable targets for individual growth and development.

Classroom observation

Study F outlines how mutual classroom observation was introduced in the context of a staff development programme. In order to gain acceptance of the idea the purposes of the observation were left to be negotiated by the staff concerned and the study demonstrates how important it is for this type of initiative to be founded on the trust of colleagues. Even with an established staff it took time before the teachers concerned felt able to share their classroom problems with one another and began to identify aspects of their classroom practice on which they would welcome feedback. The fact that the teachers engaged in observation and were themselves observed enabled them to empathize with their colleagues during the analysis stage.

Whilst classroom observation has a long established position in the field of research, it has yet to become a feature of everyday life in schools. Managed sympathetically by Headteachers who are aware of the complexities involved, it has much to offer in the context of staff development. Many programmes involve participants in the observation of individual pupils in order to make staff more aware of factors which relate to the quality of learning experiences being offered to children. This type of enquiry, together with others, such as observing pupils during group work, brings teachers nearer to the role of researchers. These types of activity enable questions to be raised about aspects of practice that have been taken for granted. They also promote interest in the complex skills of classroom observation. Once agreement has been reached on classroom access it is important for the purposes of the observation to be clearly stated since such purposes significantly influence the selection or construction of appropriate observational frameworks and techniques. It is usually better to start by using relatively simple techniques than to attempt to apply complex methods which may jeopardize the whole enterprise. Classroom observation provides a good example of a developmental activity which:

- Focuses on key issues of teaching and learning selected by participants.
- Promotes collegial enquiry and gives relatively quick indicators of changing values.
- Encourages the acquisition of requisite skills.
- Promotes critical reflection on practice.
- Increases the likelihood of constructive engagement in the monitoring process.

The outcomes of classroom enquiry cannot be wholly predictable and leaders of such initiatives need to be able to cope with ambiguity and deal constructively with unanticipated outcomes. Many observational initiatives are understandably couched in terms of confidentiality at the beginning of the process, when trust is being established, but it would be increasingly difficult to harness the results of classroom enquiries to improvements at the level of the school were this to remain the case. Every opportunity should be taken to bring about integration between the professional development of individual teachers and the achievement of corporate goals.

Many teachers become anxious at the prospect of classroom observation since they associate it with the attribution of value-laden labels such as 'formal' or 'informal', 'didactic' or 'pupil centred', slogans which were reinforced by the distorted reporting of Bennett's (Bennett, 1976) research by the media in the late 1970s. In adopting classroom observation as a basis for developmental work it is preferable to conceptualize teaching in ways that are relevant to the purpose in hand. If, for example, developmental efforts are aimed at constructing a policy for teaching and learning, one way forward might be to identify the range of approaches used by teachers in a particular curriculum area. Assuming we agree that teaching is a deliberate act aimed at bringing about learning of some kind, lessons or planned activities can be viewed as being comprised of episodes which are 'managed' by the teacher. In 'managing' the multifarious episodes that make up lessons the teacher is engaged in three core activities: monitoring, evaluation and decision-making. In making the decision to do 'X' rather than 'Y' as a consequence of evaluating pupil response, teachers draw upon their repertoires. By teacher repertoire is meant all the knowledge, experience, skills and understandings which assist the teacher in making decisions in the range of curriculum areas they are required to teach. By conceptualizing teaching as a decision-making process, a key criterion which an observer might use in giving feedback is the *appropriateness* of the teacher's response. This response should reflect agreements on how teaching and learning should be characterized in the curriculum area concerned. In this way we are able to escape from simplistic value-laden notions of 'teaching style' in favour of the idea that classroom observation in the context of development is about the extension of repertoires through collegial enquiry. The approach outlined here demonstrates the importance of careful planning and the value of using or developing a conceptual model of practice as the work proceeds.

Catalysts of change

Study G illustrates how quite modest shifts in practice can have quite extensive effects on a school. The Headteacher had sufficient confidence in his staff to delegate to the year-teams the authority to make decisions regarding the curriculum newsletter that each year group was to produce for parents. The study also indicates the varying degrees of commitment held by teachers at the beginning of the exercise. One teacher was sufficiently committed and confident on matters of curriculum policy to call a meeting for parents. Only one year group went for early implementation. After the success of that year group others followed. What we see here is a classic pattern of adoption. The strategy of letting early opinion leaders make the running helped to maintain commitment to the idea and presumably also made the process easier to manage. Attention was paid to monitoring the initial impact on first-year parents and there is ample evidence in the study of unanticipated consequences which then had to be dealt with (for example, the lack of balance within the curriculum; the need to change methods of record keeping; how to link the initiative with the school development plan; the problem of repetition in the content of newsletters). The stimulus to all these activities lay in the selection of a deceptively simple target (let's inform parents about what we do so that we can develop a school–parent partnership) which resulted in a great deal of developmental activity within the school.

Developmental opportunities and mentorship

The final study in this section centres on Deputy Headship. Not all Deputies aspire to Headship, nor will all who do so achieve preferment. The developmental needs of career Deputies in the Primary School are often marginalized since it is assumed that, as Deputies, they will be heavily engaged in the running of the school. Whether this is the case depends upon the degree to which the Head is willing to delegate authority within the school. The concept of planned developmental opportunities for Deputies arose out of work the writer had undertaken with primary Deputies, which involved the analysis of the range and variation in the responsibilities accorded to them in their schools (West, 1987). This led to a conceptualization of Headship in which Head and Deputy are regarded as co-equal partners who, through the process of mentorship, refine in each other the capacity for critical reflection. Headship was further analysed into key skills and competences which underpin the arts of Headship. The latter were defined as *connoisseurship* ('knowing how to see, to look and to appreciate' (Eisner, 1976) and the art of *educational criticism* (the ability 'to portray the relevant qualities of educational life') (Eisner). Conceptualized in this way, Deputy Headship becomes far more than the sum of the list of tasks set out in a traditional job description and more than the acquisition of skills and knowledge which may benefit the Deputy in some prospective Headship.

The developmental opportunities offered to deputies under this model require clear targets that have been agreed by the Head and Deputy and which are set in a realistic and manageable time scale. Having estimated the maturity level of the Deputy in respect of the main skills and competences likely to be brought into play, it is necessary for the Head to talk these through to assist the Deputy in making a positive start. Opportunities for the Deputy to gain further insights exist in the form of mentor style meetings when progress towards the goal is discussed. It is important that the Deputy retains ownership of the developmental opportunity and also accepts responsibility for the management of any unintended consequences that may arise. At the end of the planned opportunity, which may or may not have been successful, the Headteacher should arrange to debrief the Deputy. During the debriefing meeting both Head and Deputy should engage in the process of identifying key issues which have arisen and then go on to examine any implications of these.

The importance of monitoring and evaluation

In the introduction to Section 2, reference was made to the way in which DES Circulars and Notes are stressing the need for careful evaluation of developmental initiatives. The existence of a written policy on staff development provides a reference point and reminds us that we need to distinguish between the evaluation of the policy and the evaluation of particular programmes. The monitoring and evaluation of a programme is concerned with disclosing whether we did what we said we would do and then engaging in the collection of data and information regarding the programme. Evaluation is concerned with the making of judgements on how far the programme was effective in meeting its declared intentions together with data on unintended outcomes. It is therefore important for an agreed brief regarding monitoring and evaluation to be included in the design stage of the programme. Such a brief should also outline the resources to be used in monitoring the programme, the methods to be used in the collection of data, and identify the range of people who will be called upon to provide their perceptions of the programme in action. Methods may include interviews, the use of questionnaires, time diaries and observation, together with the analysis of documents and pupils' work. It is preferable for the individuals engaging in evaluation to use key questions identified by participants rather than restricting themselves to what they deem to be the significant aspects of the programme. The most difficult part may well be during the collection of data relating to the effects the programme has had on actual practice. Clearly, much will depend on the aims of the particular programme here and the level of detail that is deemed appropriate. If, for example, evidence was required to support the claim that a programme had increased the amount of investigative work being undertaken across the school, it would be relatively easy to establish the degree to which this was or was not the case. If, however, the programme was aimed at improving the quality of investigative work being undertaken then this would be much more complex. The Headteacher has only limited resources available to commit to the evaluation of pro-grammes. The biggest single resource available would probably be the use of the Headteacher's time, for they are usually the only individuals available in the school to facilitate the release of staff to engage in monitoring and evaluation. The potential of teacher self-evaluation should not be overlooked however, for it is possible to integrate such an approach with normal teaching. Some schools have found self-evaluation linked to peer audit a very effective way forward, particularly when programmes have been aimed at improving the match between the espoused curriculum of the guideline and the curriculum-in-action. Engaging in evaluation is of course a most productive staff development activity in itself, since it is esentially action learning. Time invested by the Headteacher in establishing a climate of trust and willingness to take intellectual risks might well be followed up in such a way. Monitoring and evaluation are complex processes which are challenging even to professionals who engage full time in the role. Schools are now beginning to pick up that challenge.

References

BENNETT, N. (1976). *Teaching Styles and Pupil Progress*. Shepton Mallett: Open Books.

EISNER, E. (1979). *The Educational Imagination*. West Drayton: Collier MacMillan.

WEST, N.F. (1987). 'Acting headship in the primary school – some management issues'. *Education*, 3–13 March 1987. Harlow: Longman.

Section 3 Policy and the Management of Resources

Introduction

We asked the Heads contributing to this section to look at the relation between the school's current needs and the deployment of resources to meet these needs. We sought specific examples of the formulation and development of a policy leading to planned change and the redistribution of resources needed to implement that change.

Study J

This describes the opportunity to participate, from 1986, in a local management scheme introduced by the Local Education Authority (LEA). It is a very practical account of how the Head took advantage of the scheme to economize in certain directions and use the money saved to meet some of the school's perceived needs for materials and equipment.

Study K

This describes radical changes in the distribution of capitation monies within the school and between teachers. It is a story of the growth of consultation and corporate decision-making and goes on to consider the relation between the allocation of resources and the planned curriculum. It concludes with a draft of a proposed policy document on capitation expenditure.

Study L

This is a very personal account of the development of the Head's own thinking and actions, leading to the increased involvement of the staff. The Head's participation in a 20-day course and then an OTTO course at Sussex University was influential. The Head went on to initiate an in-service staff development training programme, seeking in particular to relate the responsibility of individual teachers to the curriculum as a whole.

Study M

This describes how the introduction by the Head of consultative procedures to include all staff led to the perceived need to establish the sources and extent of finances available. The study reflects the difficulties involved in relating curriculum development to financial resources and these have led to a decision to review only one area of the curriculum at a time. Certain proposed expenditure led to a lively involvement with the parent-teacher association committee. The study describes a changing situation and looks ahead to further developments.

Study J: Control of the purse-strings: a case study of a local financial management scheme

Background
School J is a County primary school of some 175 pupils aged four to eleven in a not particularly affluent urban area.

'Under the Local Management Scheme schools receive a lump sum of money to cover a large range of non-staffing expenditure. The lump sum contains provision for energy, telephones, cleaning materials, postage, etc. as well as the usual capitation items. The advantage of the Local Management Scheme for schools is that they decide their own expenditure within the lump sum…It is intended that more primary schools should enter the scheme from April 1986…'

Thus one Local Education Authority stated its aim for its pilot scheme for local financial management. The scheme would extend the areas over which the Headteacher had control beyond those covered by the longstanding capitation allowance scheme. Though no additional staffing was to be made available to operate the scheme, for a Headteacher not afraid of accounts the idea of a wider and more flexible control of resources was most attractive. Virement – the ability to transfer savings made under one Head to another – would give greater flexibility. Lower telephone bills, for instance, could mean more books for children. Every school needs more books and materials than most Local Education Authorities can supply. Already the school fund was supplementing the capitation allowance by as much as 50 per cent annually. The scheme would allow any increased efficiency in the use of resources to release funds which could be deployed for the school's benefit to meet its perceived needs.

Joining the scheme

The method for calculating the lump sum to be devolved for energy was based on the average of the previous three years' consumption. The past three winters had been hard and so the oil consumption would have been correspondingly high. This would provide a good historic basis for calculating the cost of heating the school, which was 30 per cent of the total sum devolved. Moreover, the roof space had just been insulated. It was a good time to join.

Ticking a 'yes' box was all that a Headteacher had to do to show interest in the county's scheme. Showing interest was tantamount to an application for induction and a day's training course at County Hall followed. At this induction-day some Headteachers were accompanied by their school secretaries if they were to run the scheme, others by their Deputy Heads.

Preparation

The initial briefing by the Education Department's Finance Officer consisted of a restatement of the aims of the scheme: a lump sum allocation, virement between headings, all savings to accrue to the school, no downward reassessment the following year as a result of savings, and the right to carry forward up to 20 per cent of unspent monies, or £11,000, whichever was the lesser. Outside the scheme were two largely uncontrollable variables, staffing and building maintenance.

Training, consisting of exercises in form filling, codings and headings, invoices and authorizations, followed. The procedure was not so very different from the current system. Orders were to be made in the usual way. Once delivery had been made and correct invoices received, these were to be forwarded with an authorization slip to the County Treasurer for payment. Monthly computer printouts would be sent by the authority to the school, showing expenditure to date. These printouts would be able to be reconciled with running totals. After some experiment it was decided to enter these in an 18-column A4 analysis book. Two lever arch files would contain, respectively, unmet orders and completed orders. Total commitments could easily be arrived at by adding the cost of unmet orders to the totals in the analysis book.

Consultation

As far as consultation was concerned, there was no formal requirement on the part of the Local Education Authority for Headteachers to obtain the approval of school governors in order to join the scheme. It was, by implication, considered to be part of the internal organization, management and control of the school. Out of courtesy, however, the governors were informed that the Headteacher had decided that the school should enter the scheme, and later were told of its progress and benefits. Not unnaturally, they were pleased to hear that it was working to the school's advantage.

Saving money on heating

Though there had been no requirement to consult the staff of the school before entering the scheme it was necessary to explain its principles to all members of staff to secure their general cooperation. Heat loss, in particular, had to be kept to a minimum. The image of money flying out of the window took on fresh meaning. Also expenditure on electricity, cleaning materials, repairs to equipment and telephones had to be reduced or at least held at the previous level in order for the scheme to work to the advantage of the school and for the maximum amount to be released for books and equipment. Gentle reminders were all that were ever needed, for the teaching staff readily appreciated the direct benefit to their teaching of taking care in these areas.

The main member of staff responsible for savings on oil, however, was the acting caretaker. Being thrifty, she soon understood the shortcomings of a heating timer on a daily cycle with the same programme for every day of the week, which treated Saturdays and Sundays in the same way as week days. It was agreed that she should remove the timer altogether and operate the system manually, turning on the heat on her arrival at 6 a.m. and off again or down when she left or whenever the school was sufficiently warm. In times of cold weather the heating was left on all night. The warmth of the school was not reduced – cold teachers cannot teach and cold children cannot learn – but the heat was conserved and available when it was needed. Sweltering on mild autumn days because 1st October was passed happened no longer. Nor did shivering on frosty May mornings. Heat loss was reduced by improving the closers on outside doors. This improvement came under the heading of building maintenance which was outside the local management scheme and so was not a charge on the school, though the benefits accrued to it.

Lettings

Another area which now provided an incentive for more efficient management was the letting of school premises for community use. Under the scheme the school was allowed to retain 50 per cent of the income from lettings. This was partly to offset the additional heating and lighting used. Lettings not requiring heating became very attractive, especially as the school heating system was such that there was no way of heating one part of the building without heating it all. The details of each letting were carefully examined by the Headteacher and the caretaker. It soon became apparent that all the lettings were registered as youth clubs and so paid reduced rates regardless of their membership. More strict adherence to the rules as well as more frequent lettings of the school hall increased the annual income available to the school by £760 in the first year. Throughout the first year of the scheme the Headteacher dealt with all aspects of its administration from beginning to end, ordering, checking delivery notes, passing invoices for payment and checking these against the monthly computer printouts received from County Hall and, above all, constantly monitoring expenditure.

The school fund

One decision which was made early on was to debit to the local management scheme account large items of expenditure ultimately intended for payment from the school fund. This included £1,263 for carpeting two classrooms and a stairway in the first year. At the end of the financial year that sum would be transferred from the school fund to the local management scheme account. In the meantime interest would accrue to the school fund account. In the event it proved unnecessary to make the transfer as there was a sufficient balance remaining in the local management scheme account to cover this.

Outcomes

Greater flexibility meant a very much faster response to needs. For instance, three small mobile blackboards were bought for the school's three infants classrooms direct from the manufacturer. The school still had the option to buy through the county supplies department where this was an advantage, but in this case there was none. Nor was the local adviser's permission any longer necessary for purchase of such expensive items.

At the end of the first financial year savings, especially on oil, had released £1,774 for expenditure elsewhere. This increased the effective sum at the disposal of the school from the capitation allowance of £3,730 by nearly 50 per cent to £5,504. For the school's 174 pupils this meant just over £10 more per head.

Towards the end of the first year a meeting was called by the education department's Finance Officer to resolve any problems in administering the scheme and to explain to Headteachers the method of finalizing the accounts at the end-of-year closedown. Most of the problems that came up related to the accuracy of the computer printouts, the speed of the authority's response to accounting queries and some schools' inability to save. In these latter cases, allocations based on past spending which had rewarded the inefficient high spenders had penalized efficient low spenders.

The second year

In the second year of operation, 1987–88, the day-to-day running of the scheme was delegated to the school secretary. The Headteacher merely checked payments and kept a watch on running totals in the analysis book. Having understood the procedures the Headteacher considered it unnecessary to be concerned any longer with the routine aspects of the scheme.

Expenditure went much the same way as in the previous year. Once again the school had shown a saving on oil. Unfortunately, however, as oil prices have fallen by 14 per cent, the allocation, tied as it is to consumption, has been correspondingly reduced. Consequently savings have been reduced by the same 14 per cent. As for over-spending, the Authority has shown itself generous in reconsidering inadequate allowances to the school. The allowance for maintenance of furniture and equipment was increased to cover the rental of two television sets needed for a school with classrooms on two storeys. The electricity allowance has also been supplemented by an addition to cover extra use of electric fires when the main oil-fired heating system was malfunctioning. Cleaning allowance has also been increased to cover more intensive use of the building by a special unit now housed in previously vacant rooms.

The school's window cleaning has been yet another area where there has been more incentive to seek efficiency and economy in the use of resources. In the past the school had been covered by the Authority's window cleaning contract. As the local contractor had no ladder capable of reaching the highest windows, these had remained uncleaned. Now the headteacher refused to pay for what the school did not get. Eventually a special arrangement was made for a lorry with a hoist to raise the window cleaner to the top panes. The authority made a special allocation of £330 to pay for this. The school had clean windows at last. Ironically 16th October followed shortly afterwards and the sand and dust brought by the Great Gale (1988) have once again obscured the school's fine views of the South Downs.

Freedom from the constraints of the Authority's purchasing has in one case meant that an unpopular item did not have to be bought. Overalls for cleaners supplied by the Authority consist of blue cotton-polyester coats. The cleaners find these hot and constricting and rarely wear them. Last year tabards with large duster pockets and striped in the school's colours of green and white were bought. They proved very popular. They are more serviceable, and look nicer. Of course, they are not purchased on the favourable terms which the authority's bulk buying scheme can command. But as they are simple they cost only a little more than the standard overalls.

Concluding comment

At the end of the second year the Headteacher feels satisfaction in the greater responsibility for the deployment of the school's resources which has led to greater incentives to seek efficiency and economy in their use. As a result, the benefits of more careful management have led to greater value for money and the flexibility to respond directly and promptly to the school's needs, thus further increasing the effectiveness of the service provided. The movement from the administration of centrally determined programmes to the freedom to manage local resources has made the Headteacher's job more attractive to those wanting to use their management skills to improve expenditure and deploy resources in the best interests of the pupils of their schools.

Comment

This study shows how one Head seized an opportunity offered by the LEA to exercise greater managerial control and power of choice over expenditure than formerly and suggests a number of pointers in advance of the introduction of full control under the financial delegation (LMS – Local Management of Schools) laid down in the ERA (Education Reform Act). The Head readily mastered the mechanics of the local scheme and at once tackled expenditure on heating. The key to saving proved to be the willingness of the acting caretaker to operate the heating system more economically; teaching staff cooperation was of course also essential but it is an example of the great importance that must be attached to the role of non-teaching staff as LMS progresses.

The Head went on to examine how to get the best financial outcome from lettings; this again will be even more important under LMS when 100 per cent of lettings fees will accrue to the school. The Head describes several examples of greater freedom of choice being exercised to the benefit of the school. Her concluding sentence in the study underlines the importance of management skills on the part of the Head, who first successfully exercised them herself and then delegated the day-to-day running of the scheme to the school secretary. Is this again a step in the direction required under LMS?

Questions for the reader's consideration

- How could the Head best extend this experience to meet the challenge of full financial delegation (Local Management of Schools or LMS) under the Education Reform Act?

- To what extent will (a) governors and (b) parents need to be brought into the new arrangements?

Study K: Capitation policy and resources use

Background
School K is a first and middle school (age range five to 12) of some 130 pupils in a semi-rural area.

Preparing for LMS

With the prospect of local finance management expanding under the terms of the Education Reform Act, it seems even more crucial that Headteachers critically review their policies for deployment of annual financial allowances from the LEA. They may have the spending power but the governors will have the ultimate responsibility. It seems likely that in most cases the opportunity to decide exactly how monies will be deployed will rest with the Headteacher, who in turn will be accountable to the governing body. This scenario seems exciting and challenging yet presents problems for the ill-informed or poorly trained manager. A Headteacher who has little or no experience of financial budgets may not enjoy the so-called freedom of holding the purse-strings, with the increased implied responsibility which must accompany it. As most Headteachers probably come into the category of ill-trained financiers, it seems appropriate to focus sharply on the situation before it develops.

Allocating the capitation allowance

Using our own school as an example, we can portray the historical development of financial expenditure and how this has changed considerably to meet the different needs of the children today. In 1980, I inherited a typical established pattern of providing £x to each teacher. Each year I offered a princely sum of something in the region of £35 to the class teachers – rather like the Lord of the Manor offering the servants a Christmas bonus! I would announce the allocation. Suitably impressed and grateful, the teachers would scurry to the nearest catalogue and purchase their favourite items. Sadly this sometimes had little or no bearing on the needs of the children or the school as a whole. Inevitably, there was duplication of stock and an inherent mistrust of colleagues who might see 'my new maths equipment'! Gradually, it dawned on me that there must be a much better system.

For the last five years, certain amounts of money have been allocated to each area of the curriculum, such as £350 for Mathematics, £225 for Art and Craft and so on. Every member of staff was provided with a breakdown of the Schools General Allowance from the Local Authority. In this way, everyone saw the global sum and the particular amount for their area of responsibility. Decisions about the actual distribution of sums were reached by me after consultation with the Deputy Headteacher. This approach was a fundamental shift from the method inherited by me, whereby each class was allocated the fixed sum.

Better management

In this approach, there was a change in the balance of decision-making, which created several managerial improvements. First, everyone knew what sums were available and how the funds were apportioned. They might not agree with the amounts allocated but there was some room for discussion and manoeuvre before the final list was produced.

Secondly, as teachers were given sums for an area of the curriculum or a resource such as computer development, there was debate, argument and consideration about the needs of the school as opposed to the previous unwritten policy of fostering the needs of each class in isolation.

Thirdly, it developed improved communication, trust and sharing of resources. At first, there were difficulties, as teachers had to be weaned off the idea that they had 'lost' their class allocation. However, benefits soon outweighed disadvantages and it became policy, albeit unwritten and imposed from above.

Corporate decision-making

By 1987 staff had changed, our thinking had moved on considerably and we adopted a different approach. This took into account the weaknesses of our method where corporate decisions were not being made for corporate usage of equipment and resources. The 'My book', 'My maths apparatus' syndrome had faded, but there was a definite need for a corporate approach. Staff were invited to prepare a list of required items for the school. The ideas were collected and a typed list of all suggestions was circulated prior to a staff meeting. At the meeting, we examined the twenty-eight suggestions and agreed on priorities for purchases from the fund. Several deletions to the list were made as a result of staff explaining to others that the material was in the school already. For example, one teacher suggested that every class had its own tape recorder. In fact, we have sufficient in the school for that without purchasing new equipment.

Finally, the staff agreed on a set of priorities. Two major purchases were a very large paper-cutter (£77.01) capable of accepting wide coloured backing paper and some Quadro play equipment (£95.28) for the First School. The location of both items was left to the staff, because they need to gain access to them. Storage places were agreed by all. No particular person has been given the responsibility of monitoring the use of them. The cutter is in constant demand and has been of tremendous value for display work. At first, the Quadro equipment was used as a regular feature for all First School classes. Nowadays, it is rarely used. Certainly the older First School children who could gain much from construction and planning do not use it. It may be helpful now to discuss this with the First School coordinator to re-examine the need and deployment of this relatively expensive material.

The lively debate and group pressure on proper economic and efficient use of resources has been amazing. The paper cutter has been given a warning label by the Expressive Art teacher, who is determined that it will not be abused, will always be in the right place and therefore a valuable, reliable resource. This decision has arisen out of the idea of pooling our thoughts and expressing our needs. It serves as one example of a fundamental shift of responsibility.

There were still problems. The most obvious, highlighted by a term on OTTO, was the lack of a clear written policy. The draft of a policy document on capitation expenditure has been produced (see Appendix). Bearing in mind the changes under Section 29(b) of the Education Act 1986, I have given consideration to our current approach and a possible way forward.

At present, our governors are not involved in capitation expenditure in any way. It is clear that a corporate approach is desirable because everyone has an opportunity to 'have a say'. Also everyone in theory should know what is being purchased and take a common shared responsibility for treating resources carefully and wisely. The Deputy Head, in consultation with all staff, orders and monitors our stationery requirements. Any future policy must give consideration to these factors before successful practice can flourish and failure be eliminated.

Monitoring the relation between expenditure and the curriculum

Although we had congratulated ourselves on producing a real collegiate approach to allowance deployment there was something missing. All of our efforts could be totally misguided. We needed a check on exactly how and why finances are distributed. It is all very well having six teachers agree that we should buy 30 tennis balls, but who was monitoring the actual needs of the children? Who, in fact, was relating the expenditure directly to the execution of the curriculum? It is clear to me now that every penny which is spent must be directly related to the expressed curriculum guidelines. It may be attractive to have a modern piece of equipment but is it replacing any other item? Or is it a vital addition without which we could not fulfil our intended curriculum? It is quite a sobering thought when you have to match anticipated expense against curriculum intention. There are still some flaws in the argument. If, for example, a topic on Pond Life is developing so well that the Science Coordinator asks for more pond-dipping equipment, there is the vexed question of how such expense is justified and who can account for it. Does a negative response detract from a successful curriculum intention? There are no easy answers other than that there is a finite budget and requests must be seen in the light of a global sum. We are moving towards the adoption of the written policy with its implications for collegiate decision-making and hence shared responsibility. It is my role as manager to ensure a balance to all areas of the curriculum. Also, it is essential that there is equity in the staff room, the loudest voice should not demand the highest sum, nor should the core curriculum areas outstrip the other areas so that Health, PE, and Drama become the shabby poor relations.

The way ahead

The day has nearly arrived when staff will prepare their forecast with a statement of resource requirements set alongside their plans. For each teacher to produce a clear budget adequate and ap propriate training is needed. As a manager, I must ensure that this is provided. So far, no serious conflict or fundamental opposition has occurred.

The pace of managerial change is significant. Too fast a change can create confusion and uncertainty and bring criticism because of a superficial grasp of the intentions. It has been an evolutionary change, so that everyone has been aware of the process and its implications for each person. How those implications were perceived is not clear. There is clearly a need to retrain teaching staff so that there is an understanding of needs analysis related to the curriculum implementation. One step towards this is the creation of a written policy (Appendix). This is a transitional policy. Already it is evident that a much sharper focus should be placed upon the linkage between curriculum policy and needs analysis. Guidelines and procedures should be established to give direction on exactly who identifies the resources required to match the intended curriculum together with ways of monitoring subsequent use in a sensitive way. On the one hand, teachers are very busy and might see evaluation as a burden. However, on the other hand, they are often in the best position to comment upon curriculum implementation with current data about usage. Trust and honesty are essential so that proper financing is created as a way of life in any school.

Appendix: Policy document on capitation expenditure

The overriding feature is that consideration must be given to a need for resources in order to implement the intended curriculum.

1. At least once per year, all staff will be involved in the selection of all resources for the school. This selection will include basic day-to-day stationery requirements as well as major items.

2. All staff will be responsible for careful use of resources.

3. All staff will be responsible for taking care of resources and reporting damage, deficiencies and any relevant matters to the Deputy Headteacher who will assess appropriate action to be taken. Evaluation of user-rates should be carried out so that decisions can be aided by evidence.

4. The Deputy Head will be responsible specifically for stock-checks and ordering stationery material.

5. The Headteacher will be responsible for giving an annual account of School's General Allowance (SGA) expenditure to the governors.

6. Staff with areas of responsibility should present draft orders for new or replacement items to the Headteacher.

7. The school secretary will prepare and send orders for items.

8. The Deputy Head will be responsible for notifying staff of the arrival of items.

9. The school secretary will check items on arrival and distribute to the appropriate teacher in conjunction with the Deputy Head.

10. In all matters, the Headteacher has an opportunity to veto any orders, where it is deemed that there are insufficient funds or a greater need for replacement items.

Comment

This study describes the changes over a number of years in the ways in which capitation monies were used. Gradualness is the keynote. Stage One was the move from so much per class to so much per curriculum area. It included much greater involvement of all teachers in the processes of allocation but decisions were made by the Head. Stage Two introduced corporate decision-making and corporate use of equipment. Stage Three was to consider how to monitor the relations between expenditure and the execution of the curriculum. This is reflected in the policy document and leads to a recognition of the need for suitable staff training. The school is moving into a position of needs-led resourcing and evaluation of curricular outcomes. The head recognizes that only he can ensure a balance between all areas of the curriculum.

At present, the governors are not involved. It is likely however that as the post-1986 governing bodies address themselves to their responsibility for satisfying themselves that the curriculum delivered reflects the requirements of the National Curriculum, they will become involved in the resource requirements of different curriculum areas. Many primary schools are finding that to meet the requirements of the National Curriculum in Science, for example, new equipment is required. The role of a curriculum sub-committee of the governors is likely to become important in relation to that of the finance sub-committee after the introduction of LMS.

Questions for the reader's consideration

- How is the required training of teachers to be provided: INSET days; after school time; outside help?

- Governors now have general responsibility for both curriculum and finance. How may this affect the Head's plans and the staff consultation arrangements?

Study L: Leadership and cooperation in resourcing the curriculum

Background
School L is a growing junior mixed and infants school of some 360 pupils within the Greater London Area.

Few people would challenge the notion that schools of today have changed radically from what they were 20 years ago. As the rate of social change has accelerated, the need for schools to develop their relationships with the home, community, LEA and other interested bodies has become more apparent. Recent legislation, Green Papers, White Papers and countless reports have indicated the need for reform and, of necessity, staff, parents and governors as well as the DES and LEAs have had to become involved in policy-making and planning. The purpose of this study is to describe how I came to see the role of Headteacher as being that of a manager and the subsequent changes which followed, and are still taking place as a result, in the school.

Leadership and decision-making

I had always accepted and believed that the Headteacher was, in essence, the leader and (depending on his/her personal philosophy) that one's leadership style was a point somewhere on a line where one end was labelled authoritarian and the other democratic. In the early eighties I had moved from the rather simplistic model referred to above to one that involved more staff participation, but such participation was displayed at the level of discussion rather than involvement in decision-making. During 1984 and 1985 I became more aware of the need to see the staff as individuals with strengths and skills, who also accepted corporate goals. This change came about, I feel, partly because of the events described above, through LEA initiatives and as my understanding of the role of Headteacher developed. I had produced a document which detailed the school's aims and objectives, a school brochure, and had embarked on a policy of appointing curriculum leaders with a brief to look at existing documents and either to update or redesign them.

Introducing a school development policy

During the first half of 1986 I was given the opportunity to go on a 20-day management programme at Sussex University. The purpose of the programme was to provide primary headteachers with opportunities to reflect on their practice, to collaborate in identifying current issues relating to the management of schools and in exploring alternative solutions. A range of topics was covered including:

- strategies to enhance the quality of children's learning;
- personal management and leadership styles;
- staff development;
- internal and external relationships,

but, in addition, there had to be a commitment to a course of action. As the programme developed, ideas which I had already been considering began to crystallize and I decided on an action plan. My aim was to introduce a school development policy which would mean a series of planned changes in the management of resources both human and financial but especially in the human area.

I began by considering three questions:

1. What did I understand by the term 'the school curriculum'?
2. If my role as a Headteacher was to be that of a manager, what should my main aim be?
3. What did 'good' management imply?

The purpose behind these questions was to give myself a baseline from which I could begin to put my ideas into practice. I chose to interpret the curriculum as being the total learning experience offered by the school. I took as my main aim that my purpose was 'to improve the quality of pupils' learning experiences and enhance the quality of the work setting for all individuals in the setting called a school' (West, 1987). If I was to succeed in this endeavour then I needed to see that as a manager I made 'effective use of responsibility and efficient use of resources' (West, 1987) which were available. I realized that I had to have a plan that not only established priorities but also indicated the ways in which these priorities would need to be developed and how they would be evaluated.

Involving the staff: job descriptions

A combination of factors helped me to decide the way forward. By the mid-1980s, education was a subject which was on everyone's mind. Nowhere was this made more clear than in the DES publication 'Better Schools', 1985. Secondly, my LEA was in the vanguard for promoting educational change and development. Thirdly, curriculum review was already under way in my school, and fourthly, I had a very experienced and dedicated staff. My initial task was to provide more opportunities for them to take part in decision-making. During the latter half of the Spring Term, 1986 I called several staff meetings at which we considered current issues in curriculum development. These meetings took the form of open forums, especially when the curriculum areas under review were discussed, for example in language and Mathematics. Although several of the staff thought the meetings were not particularly useful, preferring the old system which simply involved my telling them what was going to happen, there was sufficient interest and participation on the part of the remainder for the first objective to be decided. This was to be the production of job descriptions. It was also agreed that as several of them already had curriculum responsibilities, and as I was aware of their interests and had kept a record of the discussions, then I should provide each of them with a job description. This document would then be subject to discussion and negotiation and an agreed copy would be produced by the end of the Summer Term. I should explain that we had looked at several examples of job descriptions and there was a general consensus as to what the main categories should be. By common consent provision was made for the stated responsibilities to be revised or changed through consultation between the postholder and the Headteacher and, secondly, as this was a new venture it was agreed that there should be an evaluation at the end of 12 months.

Our second objective developed naturally once the job descriptions were agreed: to what extent could the staff carry out the responsibilities outlined therein? Gradually the staff were to become aware of the implications in such phrases as:

...consultation with other staff
...ensure adequate resource provision
...provide advice and support
...liaise with other postholders
...monitor and record staff comments

Although not fully aware of it at the time, I had begun to develop a partnership model.

Developing staff participation

In July 1986 I was given the opportunity to be seconded for a term to attend a one-term training opportunity (OTTO) for primary headteachers at Sussex University. I felt it was a chance not to be missed because it would enable me to further develop and clarify my ideas on change and development. Obviously I had misgivings about being away for the better part of a term when I had only just embarked on a programme of staff development, but I, nevertheless, felt reasonably confident that the staff would carry on with the second objective. Furthermore, the very nature of the programme meant paying periodic visits to the school, especially at the start of the Autumn Term. During one of these visits I learned that the LEA had allocated three days for staff training during the year. In the weeks that followed I thought about the ways in which I could use the days to develop staff participation further. Part of the programme gave me the idea of a staff-led workshop, which I saw as being an extension of one of the areas in the job description, that is, that of the curriculum leader. Towards the end of the Autumn Term I went back to school and persuaded three of the most experienced and competent teachers to take part. I decided on three short inputs because it would be easier for the three to prepare their materials, and secondly, I hoped it would either awaken or keep the interest of the other staff. Finally, we fixed on a date that allowed them plenty of time.

I will not dwell on my term's secondment other than to say briefly what its aims were and that I felt it was an extremely rewarding experience. Among the aims were:

1. to 'enhance professional skills and extend understanding of management processes';

2. to plan and implement a 20-day course for colleagues;

3. to 'identify a specific issue relating to [my] own work setting and work on this during the Spring and Summer terms'.

Identifying a 'specific issue' in 3, above, was not a difficult matter for me because by choosing to look at school-based staff development I was, in fact, continuing the project begun a year earlier.

Resources and curriculum development

Coinciding with my return to school was the arrival of an LEA document relating to GRIST (Grant Related In-service Training) bids for resources to develop priority areas. The GRIST requirement raised another dimension of management which was the financial resource element. However this could not be developed in isolation because it is directly linked to curriculum development. The staff had already agreed that, as curiculum leaders, they would be responsible for providing me with a list of resource materials needed in their areas. Furthermore, my Deputy had offered to be responsible for stationery and other consumable materials – a role she had taken on during my secondment. Between us we agreed to coordinate the resource requirements of the curriculum leaders with the general school resource needs. The beginnings of a finance-resource policy began to emerge. What it lacked was a well-defined structure.

Fulfilling the job description

At the first staff meeting of the Spring Term we reviewed our progress to date. During the previous two years the language and Mathematics curriculum documents had been reviewed and updated. Work had also begun in a third area – that of Art and Design – partly because the school had no written scheme of work but also because the postholder had been given the opportunity to attend a 20-day course and one of its aims was to produce a working document. Secondly, each member of staff had an agreed job description. Thirdly, each one was exploring the realities of the role of postholder as envisaged in the job description, including the drawing up of a list of resource requirements. Lastly, three of the staff had agreed to lead short school-based INSET workshop sessions. These tasks formed part of the intended programme for the year which we discussed in our next two meetings. Therefore our first objective was the organization and content of the INSET day scheduled for 1st May. We also needed to evaluate and review the relationship between the written role for the postholder and the working role. In this matter I persuaded the staff that the most practical and beneficial way forward would be for me to interview them individually, using their job description as a starting point. The nature of the interview would be to review their previous year's work and try to plan ahead for next year. I also promised that before the review took place I would provide each of them with a paper with questions which they could ask themselves and which would help to focus their thoughts. This agreement also meant that my action-plan programme was on target. It was intended that the reviews would take place during the Summer Term in school time with a part-time teacher taking over the class for an afternoon in each case. Lastly, the question of priorities in curriculum review areas and in resource provision was raised and the need to draw up a planned programme was recognized. I introduced the staff to a modified form of GRIDS (Guidelines for Review and Internal Development in Schools) to use as a basis for future discussions prior to deciding on a programme. Our hope was to produce it towards the end of the Autumn Term.

Some management problems

The INSET day was a great success, with the staff enthusiastic and determined to put into practice some of the ideas and activities they had absorbed and experienced. When I proposed a second day there was full support from the staff. However, certain problems arose to which I need to refer. Teachers had misgivings about the 1986 pay award, particularly the conditions of service, and aspects of the 1986 Education Act such as teacher appraisal and the annual governors' report to parents. I felt that it was necessary for me to rethink the school's management structure. On the human side, the most serious problems concerned two members of staff who developed long-term illnesses. Unfortunately my management training commitments necessitated my being out of school for the equivalent of almost two months during the three terms. In management terms, a role conflict had begun to develop between that of being class-teacher and that of being a curriculum leader. Staff were becoming concerned about going into one another's classrooms as curriculum leaders rather than as colleagues – was the primary teacher's classroom autonomy being challenged? However we did achieve our targets by the end of the year and I was able to hand the governors a school policy document, albeit in draft form, together with proposed curriculum developments for the next twelve months. The staff review interviews were both successful and rewarding and I was able to agree targets – some major, some minor – with all members of staff. I had also bid for and obtained an additional 0.2 on my staffing allocation to be used for curriculum leaders' development. I used this time to help complete the staff reviews. I had also put a revised management structure to the staff which I hoped would lead to greater staff involvement and which took into account the changes that had arisen from the implementation of the 1986 pay award.

In reviewing these developments with staff we came to the following conclusions:

1.   we needed to develop the role of curriculum leaders gradually and carefully and seek to solve the problem of role conflict;

2.   we needed to allocate more time for them to carry out their responsibilities but linked to the school development policy;

3.   we decided to make staff reviews an annual commitment and an integral part of the policy document.

This year our main target will be to examine and evaluate the level of continuity in curriculum planning throughout the school. The development of the school's finance resource policy is still proceeding.

References

WEST, N.F. (1987). 'Key aspects of management'. Seminar mimeo., Oct. 1987.
MCMAHON, A. (1984). *Guidelines for Review and Internal Development in Schools*. Harlow, Essex: Longman.

Comment

In this study, the Head approaches the whole matter of resourcing the curriculum in a way diametrically opposite to that described in Study K: the latter began with resource distribution; the Head of School L began with a school development policy and addressed himself to curriculum development and staff development to meet the curriculum requirements. The development of a finance/resource policy came later.

Increasing involvement of individual teachers in responsibility for different areas of the curriculum, alongside their continuing responsibility for the delivery of the curriculum to their own class, led to the production of job descriptions. It laid the foundation both for staff-led in-service training and individual staff development through interviews with the Head and the negotiation of the job description.

The study shows throughout the intervention of the Head, both as leader of the moves in curriculum development and as manager of the staff training arrangements. It was the characteristic of his interpretation of their roles in the direction, not only of consultation but of staff decision-making and curriculum initiatives, which enabled him to carry through changes with staff support and enthusiasm. In this study, as in the previous one, governors have been little involved and the comments made on Study K should apply here also.

Questions for the reader's consideration

- How can the Head best ensure a proper balance between the individual teacher's class-teaching role and his or her curriculum responsibilities?

- Where are the teacher/time resources required to develop plans such as those described here to be found?

Study M: Relating financial resources to curriculum development

What are the available resources?

Background
School M is a junior mixed and infants school, with a nursery class, of about 390 pupils in a country town.

Headteachers are in business, competitively, with a product, targets and all the paraphernalia of the free market economy. Financial responsibility has been devolved to the school or, rather, to its governors. They should have seen it coming – the American model has existed for many years. We have not yet gone far down the American road, though since the passing of the Education Reform Act, schools with rolls of more than 200 are about to follow them. Local management schemes of one sort or another have been operating in various parts of this country in increasing numbers since 1950. In the context of this study I take Local management to refer to those areas previously regarded as 'Capitation' plus heating, lighting, cleaning materials, window cleaning, postage and telephone charges, equipment repairs, but not including staffing, building repairs, rates or debt charges. There can be an element of income derived from the school's share of money earned from the out-of-school letting of the premises.

Before discussing the formulation of local, that is to say 'in-school', policies for the management of resources, it might be fruitful to consider the nature of the resources currently available to be managed. Clearly, one needs to have available a reasonably firm statement of the budgetary constraints within which one is working. This may seem self-evident, but the mechanics of the Local Management Scheme as practised in at least one

LEA make basic planning and forecasting somewhat retrospective, particularly (but not exclusively) in the first year of participation. The school can predict its income in terms of Capitation, as can any other school, but when it comes to the next largest area of spending and potential saving, namely fuel costs, the picture becomes far more confused. Schools have been known to receive their budget statements for the year beginning in April as late as October of that year. There then follows a 'fine tuning exercise' towards the end of the financial year.

So the first constraint is one of external timing. The second is the element of chance. A hard winter cannot only destroy the one major opportunity for saving, but may even put a school substantially into debt for the following year. In view of the antiquity and inefficiency of the heating and insulation of many schools (matters beyond their control) this might seem an unreasonable risk for them to have to take. Local and national government do at least have contingency funds to afford them some protection. Schools do not have any such funds, at least initially.

It could be argued that in order to survive with any sort of coherent and consistent policy intact in the face of such uncertainties, it is more than ever necessary to have one's school's priorities clearly established in terms of aims and needs.

Better consultation

I inherited a school with a very clearly defined, if simple, financial management structure. Decision-making resided with the Head, in consultation with a small group of senior staff. I saw one of my first tasks as being that of extending the consultative procedures to include all staff. First steps in this direction were taken by changing the nature of staff meetings. All were invited to contribute to the formulation of the agenda, which was then circulated in advance of the meeting. Full contributions to discussions were encouraged from all members of staff and equal weight was given to their views. Decisions were minuted, with the secretaryship of meetings rotating among the staff.

This change of emphasis could only be sustained as credible if the resourcing implications were accepted. There is a limit to the extent to which staff will be content simply to air their views, especially if those views are new, without seeing any evidence of change. So this process of democratization brought with it the need to change the means by which resources were allocated. Previously, Heads of Departments and those with curriculum responsibilities had been allocated sums, arbitrarily fixed by the Headteacher, with which to resource their departments as they saw fit. In addition small sums, again arbitrary, had been given to class-teachers for minor purchases.

While we reassessed our aims, we tried to establish an equitable means of making short-term allocation according to present needs. One of the first things that became obvious was that we were by no means clear about existing resources. Periodic inventories of existing stock can be very rewarding! They can also raise questions concerning assumed priorities, when that which is now being asked for is found to be already gathering dust. It also became apparent that 'needs' are moving targets, and extremely difficult to rank in order of priority particularly when one has to adopt different criteria for allocation of funds from different sources.

Sources of finance

It might be as well to establish at this point what the various sources are likely to be before the full implementation of financial delegation under the Education Reform Act. I would identify five, thus:

1. Local Education Authority capitation.
2. School Fund.
3. Parent-Teacher Association (PTA) (or equivalent).
4. Bids to the LEA.
5. Residual money.

LEA money is the most straightforward insofar as virement, one of the key principles behind early moves towards local management, allows one to spend any money from that source across the range of devolved responsibilities, according to priorities agreed within the school.

School Fund money is usually quite straightforward too, in that it is often money raised by a specific event for a particular purpose or, if not, it is at least money that is recognized as belonging to the internal administration of the school to be used at the discretion of the school (though, of course, subject to audit). The only problem is likely to be in achieving staff consensus regarding priorities.

PTA money can be more difficult to administer for several reasons. It is relatively simple if the fund consists only of money raised with a defined objective – a swimming pool or a playground bench. It becomes more complicated if one enters the realms of 'educational visits' or other contentious areas. Who should be subsidized, or who should be paying for this or that activity or piece of equipment, are difficult enough questions in themselves, but when complicated by the fact that others are raising the money for the school to spend, the whole business of purse-strings can become crucial.

Bids can refer to a range of sources. The LEA may invite bids for furniture and equipment, for Information Technology hardware or minor improvements to buildings. There may be local charities which invite annual or periodic bids for funding for a specified range of educational activities, or one may wish to apply to a national or regional body for help with a particular project. The main difficulty with such sources of money lies in their unpredictability, both in terms of the likelihood of the bid being successful and also in the length of time likely to elapse before a decision becomes known.

By 'residual money' I mean that which one succeeds in saving; money that was not there when the policies were originally set, but which then becomes available and requires decisions. It can also be money which is unexpectedly allocated late in the budget cycle. Two such sums have come my school's way during the last financial year.

These then are the sources of funds for local management at present. They have to be set against the aims and needs of the school, as perceived by the various interested parties and, as I intimated above, appropriate sources have to be matched with appropriate spending priorities.

Funding curriculum change

The tensions surrounding policy decisions, and the attendant funding implications, are becoming extremely complex. Any change in emphasis, in curricular terms, carries financial implications. We have been required in recent times to absorb, and respond to, a ceaseless flow of DES documents covering almost all areas of the curriculum and at the same time we are being required to share responsibility within a far wider management structure and to be accountable for our decisions and their outcomes in a manner never previously envisaged.

Such tensions make it necessary to be both clear-sighted and steadfast in the identification and maintenance of policy aims. More particularly they make it essential that one is not pressed into precipitate action in response to the latest initiative, to the detriment of existing priorities.

The theory, in my school, is that we review one area of the curriculum at a time. This is a process which may well take up to a year to complete for each major curriculum area from identification to implementation, with evaluation to follow. Such a review takes the form of the appropriate curriculum coordinator leading a small committee which examines current practice within the school in relation to the latest professional advice, and reports back to the whole staff. Proposed changes are considered and it is at this stage that financial resourcing implications become an active ingredient. These having been identified, the proposals outlined by the staff, guided by the committee, are put to the governors. Either at this stage or earlier we would envisage a half- or whole-day closure to secure our plans for the implementation of the new policy. At some stage after this, when the staff felt confident in relation to the new policy and its attendant new materials, we would undertake some form of parents' meeting to introduce the changes to them.

Parental reactions

That is the theory, which has to be seen in relation to all the constraints that have been touched upon thus far. No new policy can be introduced in isolation, nor can decisions regarding the financing of such change be made without impinging on other decisions. Perhaps I can best illustrate these complexities by reference to two specific examples from my school.

The current review of Mathematics has brought to light the need for a substantial increase in the number of calculators required for classroom use. Accepting this need as a matter of high priority, the staff proposed that calculators were placed high on the 'shopping-list' which is maintained for reference to the PTA. When this was put to the next PTA Committee meeting a lively debate ensued on two fronts. First there was the inevitable question as to whether this was an appropriate use for PTA money, then there was a short-lived discussion on the whole question of children using calculators in class. This was brief because I intervened to make the point that the PTA committee was not the forum for such a discussion, and that the staff would be happy to explore the classroom use of computers with the parents at a future curriculum evening. In the light of the parental unease about using their money in this way, and particularly as the use of calculators is specifically endorsed both by HMI and LEA advisers, I had to consider whether I should not rather be trying to persuade the Authority to pay on this occasion. The only disadvantage would be that a decision for LEA funding would not be made for some months. One other alternative remained. I could use some of our hard-won School Fund.

Similar questions have surrounded our recently identified need for a substantial updating and enlarging of our supply of 'Home/School reading books'. One faction of the PTA feels strongly that the LEA should take responsibility for this and that if they, the parents, pay out on this occasion they will be called upon to do so increasingly in the future. The other view is that the parents want the best for their own children now and they are not prepared to sacrifice their short-term needs in order to make political points.

One section of the staff see this need for reading books as taking precedence over all others and would seek to block moves to spend any money on Information Technology until the books have been bought. Another view is that the book buying will have to be phased to allow for developments in other directions. I see my role as Head to be that of arbitrator between such views, with the responsibility for taking any decision to the governors for ratification.

The way ahead

Such questions will continue to arise throughout the year and very probably some of them will carry unexpected financial implications. From this year we shall try to reduce the areas of financial doubt by having a full staff budget planning meeting at the start of the summer term to cover the following academic year. At this meeting we should be able to present a 'profit and loss' account for the previous financial year together with estimates for the coming year. We should by this stage know our teaching staff numbers for the following year and therefore be in a position to plan on the basis of class needs as well as overall curricular needs.

Comment

In this study the Head starts with an assessment of the monies available from different sources. Further consultation with staff led, among other things, to a recognition of the need to examine carefully existing material resources, including the extent of use. The need for curriculum development being recognized, the key decision was to proceed with caution: to deal with one curriculum area at a time. Nevertheless, the requirement to deal with the budget as a whole called for decisions about needs and priorities, decisions made in consultation with the whole staff and taken to governors.

In relating sources of finance to curriculum development needs, the Head recognizes the importance of carrying parental support in using money raised by parents. The semi-political divide among parents between those willing to support the financing of educational needs and those arguing that the LEA should provide enough for all such needs has to be taken into account by the budget makers.

Questions for the reader's consideration

- In seeking additional resources, what help might be looked for from: (a) parents; (b) governors; (c) local businesses?

- In the whole enterprise of resourcing the curriculum, how should the Headteacher see his/her own role: leader? manager? arbitrator?

Commentary on case studies J to M

The Headteacher's role explored

Each of the case studies in this section illuminates the role of the Head and illustrates his or her attitudes and actions as leader of a team and manager of resources. Head J seizes an opportunity and in a combined leader/manager role effects an improvement in resources to meet needs she perceives. Her circumstances are fortuitously fortunate and she enjoys additional help from the LEA to meet some fresh needs. The remaining three Heads found themselves in positions where they needed to examine and develop their own role in order to bring about changes leading to the more effective use of resources in relation to curriculum needs. There is still, among Primary Schools generally (as distinct from our four 'contributors') a spectrum of leadership behaviour in relation to the distribution of those resources over which the Head has control. There are schools in which the limited money available is in essence spent by the Head, with some amounts allocated to class-teachers. In other schools, perhaps on the whole larger ones, the Deputy Head, the Head of the infants section in a Junior Mixed and Infants school, a small management team of some kind, share in at least giving advice and at most in taking part in the decision-making. Midway along the behaviour spectrum, consultation extends to teachers responsible for particular areas of the curriculum. At the opposite end of the spectrum, there are shared decisions by the whole staff about the distribution of resources and shared responsibility for their use, with the Head acting as guide and leader in the achievement of consensus and manager of the arrangements for monitoring outcomes. Our case studies bring out, among other things, the importance of proceeding without undue haste in moving along the behaviour spectrum and the recognition that finality is not to be expected. Nevertheless, a stage is to be expected when policy will be formalized in a written paper.

Material resources

A major responsibility of any manager, whether of a school, a service, a shop or a factory, is to assemble and keep up to date a factual analysis of the resources available. Yet it is not unknown for a Headteacher to complain to his governors that he has insufficient money for books, materials and the like, but when asked what are the specific un-met needs, to be unable to give the governors a convincing answer. More than one of our case studies show that initiatives taken by Heads to involve staff more fully in the deployment of resources have led to a more accurate picture of what already is available. Requirements indicated by teachers when consulted have been shown to be capable of being met by equipment already in the school, perhaps 'belonging' to one class or one curriculum area. Head M addresses in his contribution the importance of a proper analysis of sources of finance available, showing the unpredictability of some sources and the limitations on expenditure arising from the nature of the resource. *Ad hoc* financing by the LEA, for example, on minor works, can only be spent on certain types of items. Equipment bought from funds raised by parents has to be on items perceived by parents to be appropriate for funding by them. The complaining Headteacher postulated earlier is not always wholly frank in his discussion with governors, preferring to regard the school fund, as distinct from the capitation monies, as a separate resource available to him to use as he may think fit. The local management schemes initiated by some LEAs in a limited number of schools have been valuable stimuli to Heads to make a much fuller and more careful analysis of the sources of money available, the existing material resources of the school and the more effective allocation and use of these resources.

Human resources

More than one of our studies looks at this, though in a rather indirect way. There is increasing recognition that the special knowledge, skill and understanding of an individual teacher in a particular curriculum area constitute a resource which, when drawn upon, can considerably enhance the effectiveness of the use of material resources. There is an important inter-relationship between the managerial skills of the Head, the use of individual teachers' expertise and the allocation and use of resources. Head L sought to agree job descriptions with individual teachers, seeking to relate teachers' responsibilities to particular curriculum areas and thus to enable them to identify resource needs for those areas. Teachers' time and teachers' expertise are resources to be used with care and forethought.

How does a school best take advantage of the subject interest/expertise of a particular teacher? Part of the Head's role is to help the teacher to develop sufficient confidence in his or her ability to take the lead and help colleagues in their teaching in the area concerned. The teacher needs time to develop his or her epth of understanding of the subject area and to relate this to existing LEA guidelines and those of the National Curriculum as they appear. Some release for in-service training will help. An indication that the teacher is well aware of the need to learn herself will help colleagues to accept the stimulus and the advice offered. The Head will need to think carefully about time being made available for discussion of proposed developments. The teacher/time resource will be in part out of school hours and on in-service training days. Arrangements which allow a subject specialist, working in practice almost wholly with her own class, to spend at least some time with other classes, if possible with the class-teacher also present, need careful planning as well as tactful introduction. This dissemination stage must be followed by the process of evaluation in which all need to be involved, with again, leadership from the specialist and management by the Head.

A number of studies have examined the ways in which teachers spend their time. In this, every teacher has a management role and needs to reconsider the ways in which the precious resource of teacher-time is used and to evaluate the relative effectiveness of different sorts of use. There is a critical relationship between style of teaching, use of teacher time, the introduction of new material resources and the use of pupil time. In particular, the results of the introduction of computers in altering the balance in each of these four areas needs to be monitored and evaluated. What is lost and what is gained from pupils spending time with a computer against the ways in which that time was used before the computer arrived?

Meeting curriculum needs

Three of our four contributors to this section have chosen to describe changes in the way in which resources were allocated. In all three, the move has been towards fuller consultation with members of staff and increased attention to the needs of particular areas of the curriculum. Attention is drawn in one of the case studies to the importance of training for Heads and members of staff in both the decision-making process and the monitoring and evaluation of outcomes. Heads have found tasks undertaken within a management training programme useful and have experienced the value of days set aside for school-based in-service training. Head K sees the need for monitoring the use of resources and is at the stage of having a draft document on capitation expenditure. One would hope that future plans would look at all resources, as Head M has done, as a basis for decisions on expenditure. It is significant that increased consultation subsequently led to some feeling of role-conflict on the part of some teachers, in so far as the teachers recognized that the request for class-based resources was in competition with those sought by the same teacher for school-wide curriculum development. Heads recognize the need to move slowly rather than to expect too much too soon; Head M plans to review one area of the curriculum at a time.

Our contributors have provided accounts of the sort of changes in the direction of greater openness, more consultation and curriculum development which have been taking place over many years. Yet there is no doubt that the old-style class, cocooned within four walls, the teacher with 'my class', 'my books, my materials' and so on is still to be found in Primary Schools up and down the country. It is to be hoped and expected that the close personal relationship between teacher and pupils in the class will be maintained. But it is a quarter of a century since open-plan Primary Schools began to be built and few classroom doors are now kept shut against the influence of curriculum guidelines, advice, help and cooperation between colleagues. More recently, specific, funded, arrangements for in-school training appear to be resulting in subtle changes in role and practice. Similarly, the introduction of much more rigorous thinking about resource use, in times when very many schools, Heads and individual teachers feel that the resources provided are less than adequate, is helping to break down class isolation. As our contributors have shown, it is part of the Head's managerial role to ensure a right balance between the decisions about resource allocations. When, by job description, every class-teacher has also beyond-class responsibility, then each will face the dilemma of the choice between class-based and curriculum-based expenditure.

There is and should be a response to this dilemma, and indeed to the whole matter of resource allocation, which goes deeper than we have so far expressed. For the most part, schools generally are still in the business of budget-led resourcing. How much have we got and how shall we share it out? But the logic of meeting both curricular and class-based needs is *needs-led* resourcing. This means identifying the un-met needs in all areas of the curriculum and ranking these needs in order of priority. Such a process of working towards decisions allows a particular type of expenditure, such as that based on funds raised by parents, for example, to be incorporated within the overall assessment of priorities. There is then required a process of monitoring and evaluation which again goes deeper than is normally the case. This requires an attempted forecast of the effect of the use of the new resources being proposed, upon the use of and indeed the need for all the resources already existing. The in-school time available for learning experiences is finite. If new forms of learning experience, made possible by new resources, are introduced, other learning experiences will occupy less time and this may at least diminish the need for the direct replacement of some older resources, whose shelf life will increase. Such changes need to be monitored as the newer materials are introduced, both in relation to other material resources and to the resources of teacher-time and pupil-time. Equally the effectiveness of the curriculum development itself, with the new resources being used, needs to be evaluated in educational terms, the *educational* outcomes being assessed, and the unintended outcomes being identified as distinct from the monitoring of the resource-usage in a narrowly literal way.

External relations

Two of our contributors have been involved in local management schemes made available by the Local Education Authority and to that extent changes have had a major external stimulus. But the account of what has taken place, in all four cases, is essentially an in-school story. Governors have been kept informed but do not appear to have been involved in any real sense. The long tradition of governors leaving it to the Head to spend the money provided by the LEA continues to be maintained and this suits both parties. But times are changing and the 1986 Act has begun to affect the situation. In some schools, Heads have told governors that they are short of money for books or materials. Governors have included a reference to this in the statutory annual governors' report to parents and, while the meetings have not for the most part been well attended, the matter has given rise to lively discussion among those present. Parents are very ready to urge governors to press the LEA for larger capitation sums. This kind of development seems likely to grow with the reconstitution of governing bodies in September 1988, but to be overtaken by the major changes resulting from the Education Reform Act. Meanwhile, discussions at annual parent/governor meetings have in some cases shown an interesting split in parents' views. There are those who argue that children's needs must be met and that parents should be asked to subscribe so much per term or per year to help cover the apparent shortfall. Others argue that this simply reduces pressure on the LEA to do better and that regular parental subsidy is contrary to the whole system of LEA responsibility for education expenditure. Such parents, however, are generally supportive of fund raising efforts to meet special needs, whether for particular equipment or minor improvements of other kinds. There is here, indeed, a microcosm of a philosophical divide between the self-helpers and the State reliers which will not be resolved at the lowest or the highest level.

The Education Reform Act

For all primary schools with over 200 pupils (and, by special arrangement, for some under 200) the Act has brought about, within the lifetime of the new 1988 governing bodies, a very great increase in the resources to be distributed at school, in particular, of course, with the inclusion of all staff costs. The kind of developments described by our contributors in this section should prove to be a valuable experience in preparation for the major changes to come. Heads and governors will have had an opportunity of being consulted by the LEA on its proposed scheme of financial delegation. The way in which teaching staff costs are met, in relation to such matters as the cost of maternity leave, of long-term supply cover and incremental drift of salaries, will be critical for the smaller schools. It is not to be expected that there will be significant changes in the allocation of resources between teaching staff, non-teaching staff and material resources in the short term but it will not be long before occasions arise which call for consideration of priorities at the margins of each of these blocks of expenditure. When this occurs, it seems likely that governors, including as they now do more parents, will be involved rather than informed. In preparation for such developments, Heads and governors will be wise to prepare for detailed discussions in one or more sub-groups of a specialist character. In particular, an overall resource allocation sub-group will almost certainly be required to go into the details which will affect the finance requirements of the main sectors of expenditure.

The introduction of the National Curriculum with pupil assessments at seven and 11 will not, in our view, override the necessity for the curriculum developments already occurring, nor in any way diminish the need for the kind of resource planning we have been considering. If the National Curriculum requirements are reasonably broad, the school's essential responsibility for the delivery of the curriculum, for the actual learning experiences of the children, will remain as at present. But the indicated arrangements for the pupil assessments will require more time from teachers, notably for the moderating meetings between schools. Moreover, all the studies already published agree that the financial delegation will require increased time to deal with administrative and accounting matters, calling for skills of a bursarial nature. An early consideration of these new needs will quickly call for review of the financial resources for the major blocks of expenditure. In addition, the extra calls on teachers' time will call for a parallel and equally important review of how their time and that of their non-teaching colleagues is actually spent. Will there still be both the time and the goodwill to enable the consultation processes needed to achieve consensus to be sustained? Is it a situation in which the Head's managerial skills need to be deployed within his, or her, leadership role and style, which must be acceptable to be effective.

During the period leading up to financial delegation, the Head and governors will be called upon, as they have been already, to make decisions about above main-scale payments to certain teachers. It seems likely that governors' interest in the curriculum will be increased by reason of the consideration of resource needs for curriculum growth and the related responsibilities of individual teachers for curriculum areas. There will certainly be those among the governors who will wish to see that teachers additionally rewarded give value for money.

Section 4   The Head, the School and the Community

Introduction   We asked the Heads contributing to this section to look at the leadership role of the Head within the school itself and in relation to the wider community. We sought examples of developing relationships with parents, governors and possibly other schools, and with the officers and advisers of the Local Education Authority. Aspects of these relationships have been developed in our introductory chapter. In the event, three of our four contributors chose to look specially at links with parents.

Study N   This study describes the formation of a pre-school group for parents and children with the objective of creating a partnership with parents in the educational development of their children. The LEA provided extra resources for the formation of such a group. The Head in this case study describes some management issues arising and the Head's own role in providing the best kind of supportive environment.

Study O   The writer describes how, following her appointment five years ago, she set about developing a partnership between herself/her colleagues and the children's parents. She describes her personal accessibility to and relations with parents and the plans made for greater parental involvement with the school. Active involvement of parents with class-teachers developed especially in relation to the teaching of reading. The school has reached the stage where a written statement of policy seems to be the next step.

Study P   This describes the setting up of a sex education programme in the school and the consultation processes involved. Since 1984 the school has been involved with the Health Education Council's Primary School project and its team at Southampton University. Children, parents and teachers responded to a questionnaire; the results led to a decision to undertake a consultation process with a view to formulating a sex education programme. This has now been approved by governors and is subject to further annual review which keeps new parents informed and allows for the programme to be modified.

Study Q   The study describes the leadership role of the Head in developing the school as a community of people having common aims, interests and intentions. The direction of change has been from teaching towards learning and greater pupil involvement. The changes are described in the form of a journey – preparation, leadership, resources, planning – a journey still continuing.

Study N: 'Grasshoppers' – a pre-school initiative

Background
School N is a First School (4+ to 8+) of some 300 pupils. It serves an urban area of mixed council and private housing.

Grasshoppers might at first seem an ill-conceived name for a group which, as one of its aims, seeks to provide opportunities for pre-school children to be gently inducted into the life of the school. However it was chosen in the spirit of democracy, and I am told that members of the group saw the Grasshopper as being indicative of how one leaps into the long grass where the terrain is unknown!

Perhaps one should begin by posing the question, 'When is a pre-school group not a nursery or a play group?' The answer in our Authority would be, 'When it is an informed Pre-school Group for Parents and Children' (or PGPC as they are somewhat clumsily known). PGPC does not easily roll off the tongue, hence The Grasshoppers is a convenient name. Others in the county have names such as Acorns, Togs, Pals and other such suitable identities.

The group at our school is part of a county-wide initiative aimed at improving pre-school experiences for parents and children. In this case study I intend firstly to outline the origins and purposes of the initiative with particular reference to my own work setting. Secondly, I shall examine some of the management issues, as I see them, which have arisen out of managing such a venture. The scheme has brought a new dimension to the school and allowed to come to the surface implications for how we manage our interface with parents and the community in which the school is situated.

Origins and purposes

Our LEA has no county-wide policy on providing nursery education. There are a few nursery units but they exist largely for historical reasons and were set up to meet extreme social needs. In recognizing pressures to address pre-school needs, in March 1987 the county made proposals to establish in First and Infants schools up to 60 pre-school groups for parents and children. Hitherto there had been about 30 PGPCs operating throughout the county, but funded by a variety of other means such as Urban Aid, Further Education, Social Services and independent sources. These existing groups were generally known as Parent Education Groups and organized largely by parent educational workers who were not part of the school staffing but from Further Education establishments. The budget for 1987–88 included provision for the equivalent of 30 full-time teachers to be allocated for this purpose. The intention was that existing groups should be gently phased out and replaced by the new PGPCs, which would now be funded from primary-school staffing and as such be an integral part of the school.

At our school we were fortunate in having had a group operating since 1986 funded jointly by Urban Aid and Further Education, so the proposals were not a new idea to us.

A new initiative

Headteachers were required to make a response to the Education Officer if they wished their school to be considered for the initiative. The questions to be considered before establishing a group were:

- is the school one where, owing to the general nature of the school's intake, clear problems in terms of the language development and socialization of pre-school children is seen as a source of unusual difficulty?

- is there a classroom or other suitable space of approximately that size which can act as a base for two sessions per week?

- is the availability of that space likely to be long term? The retention of a temporary classroom solely for this purpose would not be acceptable;

- is there evidence that the school already tries to respond directly to the needs of parents and works with them?

The purpose was clearly stated by the county as being to help parents to be more effective as parents through engaging them in group work with their young children. Therefore there would be a commitment on the part of the parent to remain with their child at all sessions. This has proved to be particularly problematic as I will explain at a further point.

Clearly, having already begun to see the advantages of such a group, I felt it vital that our group should continue. In fact the initiative would provide an opportunity for expansion in terms of targeting larger numbers of parents and children. The staff unanimously agreed that we could meet the criteria and should respond accordingly. Governors likewise felt that in view of the success of our existing group, which was already feeding down the community grapevine, we should respond positively.

Thus in September 1987 the 'Grasshoppers' group was formed. The group meets on two afternoons each week in an empty hutted classroom. It is staffed by two Teacher/Tutors on equal status, one of whom is a teacher, the other NNEB (National Nursery Examination Board) trained. Both have experience in working with young children. They each have a further commitment for one morning per week to undertake home visiting to newly registered families in order to invite membership, explain the group's purposes and perhaps most significantly to introduce the school as a welcoming place. On appointing the two tutors the last was uppermost in my mind. These people would be ambassadors of our school within the community. First impressions were therefore clearly vital. The tutors are part of our teaching staff and have a contractual commitment (pro rata) under the Teacher's Pay and Conditions Act. In addition, there is an on-going professional development programme and support group to which all PGPC tutors are expected to subscribe. Professional development is organized by the County Adviser for Early Years in Education, and in our part of the county the initiative is currently being coordinated by a seconded Head Teacher. To date, there are 88 PGPCs throughout the county.

The aims of Grasshoppers are fourfold:

● to create a partnership with parents in the educational development of their children;

● to encourage parents' confidence in themselves as teachers of their children;

● to share skills with parents, to explore ways of providing materials and ideas to enhance the learning potential of children and parents;

● to create an effective link with the school and its staff and with other caring agencies when appropriate and in agreement with the school Head.

Managing the new initiative – home visiting

I see one of my responsibilities as a Headteacher as being to provide the right kind of supportive organizational environment in which new initiatives can flourish. As part of this responsibility I need to be receptive to suggestions for new ideas and practices. However, the establishment of PGPCs brought along with it the notion of home visiting, which put my receptiveness to the test.

Home visiting had been on the agenda in staff discussions for some time. Several staff members had been on courses where the notion of home visiting had been presented as a means of improving a relationship with a parent who for a variety of reasons found it uncomfortable or difficult to meet on school ground. I shared teachers' apprehension on the issue. We were concerned that home visiting would be construed as intrusive, threatening and inspectorial. Until 1987, home visiting for the group had been undertaken by the Parent Educational worker but under the new initiative the school was to be responsible for its own visiting programme. Numerous questions arose such as:

● Who should undertake the visiting?
● Should it be the Headteacher?
● If so, would I be viewed as more threatening?
● Should visitors go alone or in pairs?
● Would this new idea ruin good relationships we already had with our parents?

There were many other questions. Nevertheless, home visiting was part of the package and it had to be addressed. I discussed our uneasiness with the committee of our Parents' Association and was reassured to find that they found it quite acceptable. It was decided that initially I should not be the visitor, and that until the practice was established and accepted by the community it should be undertaken by the two Teacher/Tutors. I recently undertook a small-scale enquiry into parents' perceptions of a variety of issues connected with the pre-school group. Interestingly, not one parent had felt the home visit to be intrusive, because it had a clearly defined purpose. The tutors are now in the process of re-visiting families where there has been a disappointing attendance. I remain unsure of my role in the home visiting programme. I feel I should be involved yet am anxious not to jeopardize current successful practice by my status.

Delegation

Another issue in terms of management strategies was to decide how much autonomy the group should realistically be given. As with all initiatives in school, my policy is to ensure that participants accept ownership of that initiative, as far as is practicable. This, of course, involves delegating and giving a group of people sufficient autonomy in order to function effectively as a group. This principle then raises the question of my role as Headteacher. Delegation is not abdication, and although I decided to delegate responsibility for integrating the PGPC's activities to a Scale 2 teacher, I intended to maintain a presence within the group, reserve the power of veto (although it has never been used) and expect to be informed, consulted and updated on important developments and decisions.

However, the PGPC is somewhat unique in that its members are 50 per cent adults. Consequently, I felt it important that the group should be given every opportunity to develop their own identity, become autonomous and make, as far as is practicable, their own decisions. The group is now responding to its own needs and my role has now become that of a facilitator. The current group of parents are now arranging support meetings to take place after their children have entered school.

I have become increasingly aware that had I adopted a more 'up-front' high-profile stance this degree of autonomy, self-sufficiency and self-servicing of needs might not have taken place. The feedback I have from parents is that they find the group valuable because they can identify with its purposes and have a strong sense of being involved in its activities. Ownership has been accepted.

Parental expectations

One of the stumbling blocks in the early stages was the difficulty in explaining to parents that as part of the deal, they must attend with their child. This was a problematic area because many parents refused to join the group with such imposed conditions. Their perceptions of the group's purpose at this point were clearly misaligned with ours. Perceptions ranged from a child-minding service to a group which allowed clever children to learn to read, and 'do sums' before school. As Head, I recognized my responsibility in dispelling myths and re-focusing parental perceptions. The means of doing so were not so apparent. My staff and I had numerous discussions on how we should address the issue. We decided that the difficulty might be alleviated by giving the group a high profile within the school. We hoped that parents might feel they and their children were being excluded from something worthwhile if they refused the invitation. The Press came and took pictures. Advisers came to visit. The children, at every opportunity, were integrated for part of each session into their prospective classrooms. Children and parents borrowed books to take home and they were allowed use of the swimming pool. At the same time I, and my staff, used every occasion to engage in dialogue with parents on the opportunities the group afforded and to stress the importance we, as teachers, placed upon it. I am pleased to say attendance has vastly increased. We are now involving about 95 per cent of all registered families. Space at the sessions is frequently at a premium as babies, toddlers, grannies and even neighbours often come along with the child.

Some implications for policy – relations with parents

The DES Curriculum Five – Sixteen document states that schools, '…are more likely to discharge their responsibilities wisely when they ensure that parents and others understand their intentions and the reasons for them'. In many ways the PGPC has been a catalyst in causing us to examine our current policies on communication and relationships with parents. If we accept that a child's learning is likely to proceed more effectively by involving its most natural teacher (the parent), then we need to maintain and foster the commitment to being involved being explicitly demonstrated in our PGPC. One of the most striking anomalies arising out of the initiative is that when the child starts school, in the legal sense, the level of parental involvement/interest diminishes. For example, at a mid-term meeting in the first term of a reception class which was called by the class-teacher to explain and share with parents her work with the children, only a small percentage of parents responded. One of the Headteacher's functions as a manager is to ensure the development and maintenance of an effective communication system. This includes written, spoken and non-verbal communication. The difference in message between a smile and a tired frown can easily be interpreted or, as I suspect frequently occurs, misinterpreted. I wonder if we have coloured the perceptions some less confident parents have of school by somewhat verbose, jargonistic communication which only serves to feed feelings of inadequacy and distance. To this end our dialogue with parents is becoming increasingly less formal. We now have no formal parent consultation evenings; instead teachers are always available on Wednesday evenings after school to discuss concerns or just chat. Informal drop-in coffee afternoons for staff and parents where education is not necessarily on the agenda, educational evenings for parents which involve children and social events for parents and staff are a few examples of new practice.

Open-door policies and having parents working alongside teachers in the classroom go a considerable way towards involving those parents whose confidence enables them to respond in this manner. But what of the others? I remain convinced that the key to this widespread concern lies in the perceptions many parents have of schools, and it is the refocusing of these perceptions that is the key to a successful parent-teacher partnership.

Some teachers have made accusations of apathy and lack of interest. Many have made assumptions about the neutrality of school ground. I would agree that to many parents, who hold apprehensive and threatening perceptions of school and teachers, it is anything but neutral. I would also argue that most parents *are* interested but do not have at their disposal the means to convey this interest.

By showing ourselves open to suggestion, being attentive listeners, valuing parental views and perhaps being more sensitive to the possible reactions of parents to the messages, both formal and informal, which we send, I believe a realignment of the professional/lay boundaries can occur.

In the previously mentioned small-scale enquiry into parental perceptions the question of diminishing involvement and seeming lack of interest was addressed. I interviewed a random selection of comparatively new parents and the committee members of our Parents' Association. In the majority of responses, parents felt that they should only become involved if their child was experiencing difficulties or problems. But what of celebrating success? As a Head who subscribes to the ability of an organization to share and celebrate its successes as a positive means for learning and growth, I found this response illuminating yet worrying. Thus celebrating success with parents has now come to the forefront of school policy, the benefits of which I hope will be reaped.

Meanwhile, the Grasshoppers continue to grow, develop and flourish, not least because of the professional guidance of the two tutors. Parents grow in confidence and we are seeing children integrate more readily into the ethos of the school.

I see my role continuing to be that of the facilitator and hopefully 'interested friend' of the group. If we keep cutting the long grass it will allow the grasshopper to take a small hop, rather than a leap, into that new terrain where, of course, he will find no predators.

Comment

This study presents a fascinating account of the progressive development of relations between the Head and staff of a First School and the children's parents. The trigger for this development was the decision to establish a pre-school group for parents and children in response to an initiative by the LEA. Note that *parents* were members of the group. The establishment of two staff for this group gave the Headteacher an important decision to take: how far to delegate. Wisely she chose to do so very fully, retaining the right to be kept informed. Teachers expected some opposition by parents to home visits but these fears proved groundless; again the Head left the visiting to staff. Increased contact with parents showed that there were misapprehensions and misunderstandings on the part of parents about some of the school's work, so what amounted to a public relations exercise was begun. Gradually, formal meetings gave way to more dialogue of a personal and informal kind. The Head reached out to parents not simply to respond to problems but to celebrate success.

My own concluding observation would be that the growth of better school-parent relations is not basically about organizations but about direct personal relations between individuals: Head, teacher and parents.

Questions for the reader's consideration

- Can the arrangements for a pre-school group described here be developed even without specific planning and support from the LEA?

- What are the reader's own expectations of the extent of parental involvement with the school?

Study O: Creating a partnership with parents

Background
School O is an urban multicultural Infants School of some 350 pupils serving an area of mixed housing.

Although Sir Edward Boyle referred to parents as the fourth partner in the education service as long ago as 1963, making that partnership a reality a quarter of a century later is no easy task for the Headteacher. A partnership with parents in the educational process implies more than achieving good communications with them and exchanging information, necessary as these things are. It is about sharing in the education of their children, recognizing the vitally important role they have played prior to the start of schooling and seeking to continue it. To develop this partnership, open access to school is necessary, feedback from parents has to be encouraged and sought and time has to be invested. The staff of the school have to believe in its worth and have to feel comfortable in the role of partners rather than distant professionals, holding the balance between friendliness and familiarity.

A Headteacher's vision

When I became a Headteacher five years ago, I held certain assumptions about the desirability of parental involvement in their children's education. Parental help had been an important feature of my classroom as a teacher. I enjoyed easy communication and regular daily informal contact with the parents of my pupils. A friendly atmosphere was encouraged, in which it was easy to discuss any problems and deal with them before they grew into crises. I was used to parents coming to class assemblies to share our work and to their attendance at Open Mornings when they could spend time looking at how the class was organized and worked. Serving a middle-class area, I was also used to answering articulate demanding questions about the curriculum. I acknowledged that parents did have rights which as a teacher I had to respect. To me this was part of my professional accountability. I felt I had reached the stage where I wanted parents to be more systematically involved in their children's education because of the benefits that would accrue and were being documented in research.

My task as a Headteacher was to begin to take a school towards my vision of such a partnership, to encourage parents to become involved whilst inspiring the staff to allow them to do so and at the same time being aware of a possible cultural gap between teachers and parents that would have to be bridged.

The starting point

The school is a large (350 pupils) urban multicultural Infants School which serves an old-established council estate, modern council housing and some privately-owned late Victorian terraced houses. Parents were welcomed into the building and some helped in classrooms but there was not a positive attitude towards their greater involvement amongst many staff. Some of the staff had been there for a long time and doubted that increased interest amongst parents could be created. They felt that the kind of parents in the area were those who would be unwilling or unable to become more involved. They expected to see only half of the parents at an Open Evening. To some extent they also guarded their professional status.

When I began I determined that I would be easily accessible to parents, operating very much an open door policy which would be an example to staff. Unfortunately my office and the Secretary's are upstairs away from the hubbub of life and I wanted to be seen to be welcoming. On the other hand I felt that I looked silly and purposeless merely standing in the corridor, so I got into the habit of finding small jobs that would take me back and forth along the corridor through the two buildings whilst at the same time enabling me to speak to many parents as they brought in their children. I do this less frequently nowadays as parents know that I am available upstairs, but it is a device I maintain because it achieves quick informal contact with many parents.

Parent reaction

This openness and approachability was a contrast to my predecessor's manner and initially parents had to adjust to it. Their memories of their own frequently unpleasant experience of school and their rather aggressive approach to the authority figure of the Headteacher meant that I was not always treated in the manner I had hoped. I think it is important for the Head to be aware of and understand people's reactions, but not to be deflected from the intention of establishing the atmosphere and relationships already determined on.

Whilst developing an open school, I have to take care to maintain certain rules which we have about parental access, which the staff are keen that parents do not transgress. At the close of the school day parents are asked for safety reasons to wait in the playground for the children to be brought outside by their teachers. A few parents choose to wait inside and cause congestion in the corridors and staff expect me to perform the not always pleasant task of getting them to move outside.

The way in which I as the Headteacher dealt with and talked to parents initially was a powerful example to staff, who knew from our first staff meeting that I viewed parental involvement in education as an aim for the school and that it was necessary for us in the school to reach out and bring them in.

Class assemblies

Time has to be allowed for people to change their attitudes, but changes in practice can help in their encouragement. I saw class assemblies, which would focus on work that had been done, as a good way of informing parents and developing their interest. As there was no reporting to parents in the Spring Term I asked staff to undertake such an assembly towards the end of this term. Enthusiastic support from the Deputy Headteacher helped to offset staff worries and nervousness. I gave them ideas for possible content and support and praise for their efforts no matter what presentation was made. Attendance by parents was fairly good but not sufficient to prevent teacher assertion that parents were not interested. As Head I found it necessary to reaffirm that numbers would increase as word passed among parents. Five years later that faith has been vindicated, and parents appreciate the fuller picture they receive of the kinds of work the class has undertaken. Staff are much more relaxed and positive.

Home reading – a small group approach

Although greater parental involvement did take the form of a group who were keen on fund-raising activities to support the school, and have a parents' room as their base, my main concern was to achieve parental involvement in their children's education and I felt that Reading was the area where progress could be made. As a staff we had begun very early in my headship to consider our approach to Reading and had decided to abandon a Reading scheme in favour of storybook material and 'Story Chest'. During discussion, staff had spoken of their appreciation of the benefits of parental support at home in reading and some of them were quite keen to systematize that involvement a little more, although wondering if parents 'in our area' would be sufficiently interested to give that support.

We moved into home reading along lines similar to PACT (parents, children and teachers, the structural home-based reading scheme developed in Hackney under the Pitfield project), but I left it to individual teachers to decide on their methods. I felt that we could learn much from trying different approaches and that if I pushed all the staff to make this large commitment of time all at once, some would be resentful and the scheme would be unsuccessful. This was during the period of teachers' industrial action. When staff expressed interest I talked to them individually about meeting parents and getting started. I thought that small informal meetings with groups of parents would arouse interest and be more successful than large group meetings and I freed class-teachers either first or last thing in the day to talk to parents over coffee to explain our approach. Not all parents responded to the invitations but a sufficient number did for staff to run successful schemes.

Sharing success

Sharing that success with all staff at meetings has provided a positive impetus towards a whole-school adoption of this approach. As Headteacher I have to maintain the momentum by disseminating information of its benefits and by encouraging staff to invite parents more than once to meetings to give them the chance to participate. Failure to involve some parents has to be acknowledged but not allowed to discredit the programme. I see my role as a facilitator and active supporter.

In involving parents more closely in Reading, the problem of their conservatism and different expectations has arisen, for most of them view Reading as an event which is related to the use of 'Janet and John'. To have held a general meeting for parents to discuss the school approach would have been unproductive, but the small group meetings and informal teacher–parent contact have done more to develop some understanding of what we are doing and how they can help.

Improving parents' understanding

As we move towards greater parental involvement it will be necessary to explain even more to parents about what the teachers are doing. Greater confusion about teaching methods and content will result if we do not. Already some staff have suggested curriculum workshops for small groups of parents. As Head I am pleased that suggestions come from the staff because they illustrate a shared approach and a sense of collegiality which was lacking in the first years of my headship.

Informality of style, as David Winkley (1985) has pointed out, is often the key feature of the successful school event. Over the years this has happened more and more. The Nursery Class Open Week, when the family, grandparents and babies included, can spend an entire session if they wish, is a result of this development. I would hope to explore with the staff ways in which the school could be open during the day so that parents could see the work going on in the classrooms.

Another important step towards partnership has been the home visiting done by the ESL (English as a second language) teacher, particularly just before the children start school. She expressed interest in starting to do this and I gave her every support because it makes a link between the school and parents whose experience of schooling is very different. Many possible difficulties can be dealt with before they even arise and once again the teacher can explain the approaches and methods we use and show how they can help at home. We think our next step will be to engage Asian and West Indian teachers from the ESL Service to talk to parents about our approach to Reading.

Personal relations

Visitors comment on the friendly welcoming atmosphere they find in the school. Staff take their lead from the Head and I always try to be friendly but calm and unruffled in dealing with parents. There is a lot of value in a smile. Staff are conscious of the need to avoid talking down to parents. They see themselves as approachable and easily contacted by parents and this is borne out by comments that parents have made.

I have developed my relationship with the staff so that I can talk to them about how they might appear to parents. For example a certain brusqueness in manner does not encourage volunteer help. I spend time with probationary teachers discussing how to handle their first parents' evening. It is easy to forget how daunting that can be for young teachers and they need to realize that talking to parents reflects school policies.

The way ahead

Although we have had some successes we have not found that the number of parents involved in classrooms has increased much over the past few years. One factor we have identified militating against participation has been the growing practice of mothers to take part-time jobs once the youngest child has started school and hence be unavailable during school hours. On the other hand, perhaps we have to be prepared to accept help for a limited period of time rather than looking for a long-term commitment. I think that I could do more as the Head in this area as I know parents better than the class-teacher at the start of the school year. I could seek out helpers more actively and direct their offers to various classrooms.

I undertook an exercise by which I interviewed a small sample of parents individually to discuss the information they are given by the school and what information they feel they need or would like to have. The parents were relaxed and talked openly and frankly and a lot of very useful feedback emerged. They were looking for more information about the curriculum and suggested workshops and class newsletters as methods of approach. Their ideas can be usefully passed on to staff so that we can decide on our next moves forward.

I think that we have reached the stage as a staff where we need to discuss our approach to parental involvement and to formulate a written policy which will be evidence of our commitment to parents and to the Governing Body. We can share in the process of its formulation. Five years ago it would have been a document written by me to which staff might have subscribed in varying degrees. Now I think that we can achieve a shared ownership of our policy.

Reference

WINKLEY, D. (1985). 'The school's view of parents'. In: CULLINGFORD, C. (Ed). *Parents, Teachers and Schools*. London: Robert Royce Ltd, pp. 73–96.

Comment

As a case study of the management of change in respect of relations between Head, teachers and parents, this study shows many similarities to case study N. The Head of this large Infants School had a clear idea of the kind of development she wished to provide but there was not a positive attitude to more involvement on the part of many teachers and many parents. While individual parent help was welcome, more general relations were somewhat stand-offish. These aspects of the Head's management style and strategy stand out from her own account: lead by example; don't expect the same degree or kind of progress for everyone at once; and move from formal meetings to small informal group meetings with parents. At every stage the Head is content with small beginnings and prepared to expect gradual growth. The examples given were particularly of class assemblies, to which parents came, and home reading arrangements. The work of a visiting ESL teacher included some home visiting, another outreach to the individual parents.

In proposing the need for a written policy, the Head gives a nod in the direction of governors. The second question at the end of the study invites thought. My concluding observation is as in the previous study: direct personal relations are paramount.

Questions for the reader's consideration

- This study is in many respects a story of leadership. What are the chief factors contributing to its success?

- What part might governors and in particular teacher-governors be expected to play in such developments?

Study P: Setting up a sex education programme in school: a consultation process
The health education context

In 1984 our Junior School became involved in the Health Education Council's Primary Schools Project, one of about a hundred similarly committed schools in England, Wales and Northern Ireland. The project team, based at Southampton University, and directed by Trefor Williams held, as a central tenet, that Primary Schools should be health-promoting communities. Following from this, it sought to provide a coherent framework for health education based on the views of parents, children, teachers and health workers involved in the care of the schoolchild. It should be noted that the opinions, wishes and perceived needs of these four groups were to be given equal weight and status.

A key tool in the team's consultation process was a questionnaire based on a checklist of 43 health-related topics. This 'Just a tick' instrument was devised by John Balding at Exeter University, and it was given to parents, teachers, health education personnel and children above the age of eight. Children between the age of four and eight, and other children experiencing language difficulties, used a 'Draw and write' technique devised by the Southampton team. This asked them to draw and label all the things which made them healthy and kept them healthy. The responses fell into 16 categories, which included such topics as exercise, hygiene, and safety.

The questionnaire invited the older children to identify those topics which interested them most, and asked the adults to comment on the importance of the same topics and at which stage of Primary School education they should be introduced. The 'Draw and Write' technique simply explored younger children's perceptions of health education notions. An analysis of the results of this huge survey enabled the project team to build up a health education framework for schools which helped teachers match appropriate resources and teaching strategies to children's conceptual levels. Just as importantly, it enabled individual schools to develop a health education programme based directly on the needs and wishes of the consumers. Teachers were not enlisting the support and help of parents for a curriculum that had already been devised; parents and children demonstrably had a say in what should be taught.

Sex education – the questionnaire results

When the first results of our school's questionnaires had been returned, we had arranged for our school nurse to give a talk on menstruation to our fourth-year girls and to those of their parents who also wished to attend. In response to a letter sent out before the talk all the parents were happy for their girls to attend, and no one wanted to withdraw them for any reason. This was encouraging, but the talk was divorced from our day-to-day curriculum, ignored the needs of the boys, and its very separateness highlighted a certain unease in what we were doing.

Clearly, something more satisfactory was required, and the results of our questionnaires indicated that parents and children would welcome a more systematic approach to sex education. Out of the 43 items on the questionnaires four were of specific use to us in this area of the curriculum, these being 'how my body works', 'how a baby is made (reproduction)', 'menstruation (periods)' and 'differences in growth and development'. Adults were asked if these topics should be included, or included if there was time, while the children had to indicate if they were very interested or quite interested. The table below shows some of the results:

	% indicating yes to inclusion		% indicating interest	
	Parents	**Teachers**	**Boys (10–11 yrs)**	**Girls (10–11 yrs)**
How my body works	89%	100%	64%	75%
How a baby is made	72%	50%	61%	92%
Menstruation	70%	76%	14%	92%
Differences in growth and development	79%	75%	58%	75%

Consultation

The 1986 Education Act required school governors to keep a written record as to whether sex education should be part of the curriculum, and, if they considered it should be given, they were to state the content and organization of the teaching they would wish. This concentrated our minds, and with the experience of the Primary Schools Project behind us, we decided to undertake a consultation process with a view to formulating a sex education programme. This process was, in the event, filmed by Central Television.

– with teachers

The first part of this process was a meeting of our Junior School staff with colleagues from our Infants School. We had held such meetings for other areas of the curriculum to ensure continuity of practice and content, so this was simply an extension of a well-established pattern. The debate indicated that teachers were happy to teach about growth and reproduction, given the appropriate materials. However, while acknowledging the importance of telling children the truth, the prospect of dealing with an individual child's question such as 'How do you catch AIDS?' was one that caused concern. We have subsequently become involved in an excellent in-service training programme on Personal and Social Education run by our LEA, one element of which rehearses teachers in their responses to children's questions.

– with parents

We called a meeting with parents of fourth-year children, and showed them the films and books we intended to use with the children. Our school nurse was present at the meeting, which focused on several issues. One was that boys as well as girls should have the talk on menstruation, another that the lessons on growth and changes in boys and girls at puberty should be given before the fourth year. The third important point was that parents did not want us to deal formally with AIDS or, by implication, homosexuality.

– with governors

The other element of the consultation process was the governors' meeting. It was a joint governing body for the infant and junior schools, so looked at a sex education programme for the whole primary age range. It was agreed that the programme should, as far as possible, be integrated into an overall health education scheme, and that the formal content should go no further than growth and change at puberty, and reproduction. The questions of parents not wishing their children to be involved in sex education lessons was examined. It was suggested that formal contact be made with the parents, and that the headteachers and class-teacher explain the lessons in detail and attempt to alleviate any worries. However, in the final analysis the school could use its discretion in excusing pupils from sex education lessons.

At the end of the consultations the governors were able to agree a policy. Everyone had been given a chance to air opinions, we had talked through some difficult problems, and the written document represented shifts of emphases and attitudes as our awareness of the issues had been heightened. *The governors' statement on the teaching of sex education* read, therefore, as follows:

The governors and Headteacher will take such steps as are reasonably practicable to secure that the sex education given in the school to all registered pupils is given in such a manner as to encourage those pupils to have due regard to moral considerations and the value of family life.

The formal *content* will consist of the following:

- that living things come from living things;

- that like comes from like;

- study of mammals, reptiles, birds and so on, and the differences between them;

- animal homes and how animals care for their young;

- care of pets;

- that seeds are living things;

- life cycles and growth – for example, seeds becoming flowers, and tadpoles frogs;

- growth and changes in boys and girls at puberty;

- how babies are made;

- care of babies, and the importance of families in loving and caring for them.

These topics will be taught formally, but questions will obviously arise out of them. Teachers will answer these questions truthfully but sensitively, pitching their answers at the appropriate level. Correct terminology, and not colloquial language, will be used.

The *method* of teaching will be to incorporate the subject into the investigation studies and health education programme of the school. This will make it as natural a part of the children's curriculum as possible.

We are trying to engender positive *attitudes*. The processes of growing up, and reproduction, are wonderful ones. We are telling the children that their bodies are a great gift. They must understand them, look after them, and respect them. They must expect other people to show the same respect for them, and, in turn, learn to show warmth towards others and sensitivity towards their feelings. These attitudes are an everyday part of life in the school. Parents will be informed about the sex education curriculum, and their help and support in the teaching process enlisted.

Some problems   There are interesting considerations which arise out of the consultation process outlined earlier. There is the problem of wanting to protect childhood innocence, while at the same time attempting to protect children from the well-publicized dangers (such as 'Stranger Danger' and child abuse) that they are confronted with almost every day on TV, radio, and in the newspapers. One parent told us that, after watching one of the short TV films warning against AIDS, her son had been crying because he was sure he would die of that condition. It was a timely warning against making assumptions about children's perceptions and understanding. Again, not all children enjoy a happy family life. HMI (Her Majesty's Inspectorate) in *Health Education from 5 to 16* stated that teachers should approach delicate issues within a moral framework but recognize that many children come from backgrounds 'that do not correspond to the ideal of a loving relationship in which there is respect for others.' Faced with such children, teachers need 'great sensitivity to avoid causing personal hurt and giving unwitting offence'. This whole issue, of knowing what experiences and values children bring with them to school and how to respond to them, is a difficult one. However, it can only begin to be resolved by encouraging honest dialogue and trust between teachers and parents.

A second area to consider is the consultation process itself. This is enshrined in our governors' document and will not happen once, but every year. Parents will be shown new materials, and have teaching methods outlined, and in turn will give us their opinions. Thus, they will always have a real influence on this aspect of the curriculum. Some have said that we at school can explain 'the facts of life' better than they. This suggests the need for an extension from explanations into workshops where parents can be given the confidence and skills to take a full part in their children's learning. Projects in home–school learning links have indicated, at the least, improved attitudes to school by children and parents. Such projects suggest that we should be exploring ways of giving more ownership to parents for their children's learning.

A third point of interest highlighted by our part in the Health Education Project's survey is the idea of researching parents' wishes and opinions. This could take the form of a simple questionnaire, and, at first, could tackle such non-curriculum issues as home–school communication. The important thing is for the process to be honest, with the school showing a commitment towards necessary changes. The canvassing of opinion on particular aspects of the curriculum could be made part of individual parent-teacher discussions. Parents give great support to these private discussions on their children's progress. One of our fourth-year teachers took a few minutes at the end of each session to ask parents their opinions on our sex education programme. Many parents expressed gratitude at being given this opportunity to share views they would not have aired at a larger gathering.

The determination of a school to engage in a real dialogue with governors, parents and others in the community involves much time and effort. It would therefore be sensible for Headteacher and teachers to target four or five key objectives and spend most of their energies on these. We did this at our school and one of the objectives was, 'Parents will be actively involved in their children's learning'. Thus, staff share a common view on the desirability of good home–school links. They are prepared to be open about difficulties, and to share some of their expertise. This can be a tiring and painful process, but, in Shakespeare's words,

> Our doubts are traitors,
> And make us lose the good we oft might win,
> By fearing to attempt.

Comment

Uniquely among our case studies, this study addresses itself to *structured* consultation. Springing from the school's involvement with the Southampton University research and consultation on health education, together with the statutory requirement made under the ERA for governors to approve arrangements for sex education, the school undertook direct consultation by questionnaire with parents and pupils. To my knowledge, this is the first example of consultation with all pupils about an area of the curriculum.

The sequence of direct discussion that followed is significant: first teachers, then parents, and finally governors. The outcome was the approved governors' statement reproduced in the study. Important consequential considerations followed. Implementation of the programme made teachers aware of the need to consider reactions of individual children, a lesson of general application. Secondly, home-school learning links improve the attitude to schools by children and parents. 'We should be exploring ways of giving more ownership to parents for their children's learning'. Thirdly, the school has become very aware of the value of researching – formally or informally – parents' wishes and opinions. Significantly, after this decision about sex education, governors appear to have dropped out of the consultation process. It is for the reader to consider the questions posed at the end of the study.

Questions for the reader's consideraton

- What light does this study shed on the possibility of involving parents and governors more fully in a consideration of curriculum development in other areas?

- Given that the ERA requires governors to have general oversight of the curriculum, how is this best managed? What should be the role of the chairperson of governors here?

Study Q: Establishing a school as a community

The school as a community

Background
School Q is a Middle School (8 to 12) of some 250 pupils in a pleasant suburban area.

One of the compliments which we regularly have paid to our school is that we provide a caring, sharing community. I seek to describe here how a particular style of management has facilitated the development of industrious harmony amongst the teaching staff, and hence pervaded the whole school.

My definition of a community is that of a group of people having common aims, interests and intentions. Any true community can only attain its common core of purpose and direction through regular and lively debate, in which all can expect both a voice and an audience. The channels of communication must be explicit, open and practical in the demands they make on any individual's time and energies.

This school has 250 pupils aged 8 to 12 and a staff of 10 full-time and four part-time teachers. Our fortnightly meetings alternate between before and after school, since each of these times is preferred by certain members of staff. The dates of these meetings are set before the beginning of the academic year, and their main function is that of determining and directing our curricular aims, policies and practices.

Keeping everyone informed

Day-to-day notices, organizational matters and reminders are brought to everyone's attention in one or more of three ways:

1. a calendar in the staffroom, to which all staff can add information;

2. a notice book available before school so that anyone can enter notices therein, and circulated to all staff at the beginning of each day (especially important on the days when most staff are not present at assembly);

3. a 'This Week' list of items for the attention of all staff on our main notice board.

In all these ways the whole school is kept informed and aware of what is going on.

Similarly, assembly provides a vital opportunity for the children to keep the school informed about their successes and achievements, either individually or as members of a class or team. Such reports often relate to their hobbies and interests outside school, providing a link with the wider community of parents, home and neighbourhood. The use of the school notice board to advertise a missing pet or an article for sale serves a similar purpose.

Using an open-plan school

The school is modern and open-plan in design, with nine teaching bases and four smaller rooms around a large central area and library. The staff moved to this site from a Victorian building nine years ago, and I was appointed to my first Headship here three years later. It soon became clear to me that the scope and flexibility offered by the open-plan arrangement had not been recognized or appreciated. Classes remained in their own bases, collected their resources around them and staff allocated each small room for a specific purpose (for example, a television room).

I must interpose at this point my strong belief in the merits of an 'open' school, where sharing and accessibility relate to resources and information, to skills and abilities, to opportunities and responsibilities. In this sense, then, there are 'open' schools in antiquated buildings, and 'closed' schools in surroundings which invite and encourage the very qualities of collegiality mentioned above.

As a manager I addressed this situation in a particular manner, one which was appropriate to my position as a probationary Headteacher but which I continue to utilize with a high degree of success. I knew that change posed both a threat and a challenge to the staff; that any initial feelings of anxiety and uncertainty would be difficult to dispel. However, I also knew that such feelings would become compounded if what I saw to be necessary changes were seen by staff as unwelcome and imposed.

Learning and teaching

My starting point was a perception that the school (in common with many others) needed a change of emphasis:

- from teaching to learning;
- from teacher-direction to greater pupil involvement and responsibility;
- from whole-class teaching to a more individualized and group approach.

Education Observed (1982) – a review of the first six months of published reports by HMI said, 'Attention should be given…to the development of teaching styles which take more account of individual abilities, to the improvement of continuity and progression, to giving pupils more responsibility for their own learning, to placing more emphasis on oral work and discussion, and to relating the work more closely to pupils' own experiences and interests'.

But what HMI were consistently finding on their visits to schools was that 'whole class teaching is by far the most common method employed in schools at every level'. The question I addressed was why this should be the case, since so many teachers agree in principle with the sentiments of what HMI were advocating in the passage quoted above.

Turning intentions into action: a journey

The gulf appears to be between theory and practice; between good intentions and the excuses, the problems, the doubts which are allowed to intervene; between perceiving a need and *being able* (rather than just willing) to change one's strategies and actions to provide for that need. I wanted to change the thinking of my staff, not in any cosmetic manner, but so carefully, helpfully, certainly, that their actions would also change to mirror their thinking. I wanted to achieve my goals in the way epitomized by the Chinese sage Lao Tzu, 'The best sort of leader is hardly noticed by people. When he has finished his work, people say, "We did it ourselves"'.

I can best describe the sense of community which characterizes our school by drawing an analogy between the way the staff work together and a journey. This is no coach tour in which the customers sit back and admire or criticize that which is paraded before them, but rather a journey demanding involvement, participation and action.

1. Before setting out
Time is needed to come to know the children, staff and organization of the school. I spent my first year getting to know the styles and qualities of the staff both as individuals and as members of a team. Little was changed from the reign of my predecessor, but many questions were asked of pupils, of parents, of teaching and ancillary staff; indeed of anyone who might be considered a member of the school family. I was seeking to establish the areas

of success, strength and achievement as well as those of dissatisfaction, doubt and disillusion.

The following will give some indication of the range of concerns which this period of review highlighted:

(a) There was a clear hierarchical structure to the staff, with the Head, Deputy and one or two senior teachers making all the major decisions, without consultation, before informing the rest of the staff of the consequences for them.

(b) The week was tightly time-tabled, largely because of the degree of specialist teaching. This allowed no extended periods of class contact, especially in the upper part of the school.

(c) The building was poorly used, as described earlier.

(d) The staff were stagnating in the sense that there were few opportunities for promotion and they were firmly entrenched within particular year-group boundaries.

(e) Resources were often jealously guarded rather than pooled and shared, to the ridiculous level where certain materials could have been in school for many years without anyone other than their 'owner' knowing that they existed.

2. Lead the journey

...rather than send one's colleagues off on an unaccompanied mystery tour. Every community is dependent upon the skill, experience and expertise of a number of people, but requires leadership to blend these qualities to a harmonious whole. I had to be prepared to lead by example, and to change my views as well as expecting to change those of others. This meant my involvement as a teacher for sound, constructive reasons rather than as an excuse to evade the monotony of office work, or simply because 'I like to keep my hand in'. This teaching to show what is practical, purposeful and possible had to be seen to succeed – and hence I had to know and accept my own limitations. It was vital that I work in the same conditions I would expect my colleagues to work in, and therefore not seek the advantages of small groups, with special resources, at irregular intervals. I chose to work with a third-year Maths group in the central area of the school. My main aims were to make extensive use of practical materials to support the children's learning, to promote responsibility by allowing children access to these materials, to work extensively outside the core scheme on which the school was over-dependent, and to actively seek opportunities to relate our Mathematics to the outside environment (through visits to a local multi-storey car park, a supermarket check-out area, and so on). As one might expect, some staff followed my example more readily than others. However, as more were 'won over' there was a greater pressure on the few remaining to join the fold, and their reticence was countered by the large number of colleagues to whom they could now turn for advice and support.

I also agreed from an early date that I would willingly cover for any course which did not attract supply cover if the rest of the staff and the children would ultimately benefit. Guides were employed in those parts of the journey where their knowledge and experience would prove invaluable. In this category I would include inspectors, advisers, HMI, governors, Headteacher colleagues and teachers. It is vital to their development that one's own staff should be utilized in this capacity whenever the opportunity presents itself. I have invariably found that by taking a back seat in this way, talents which may have lain dormant for years can thrive and blossom again. A prime example would be that of an exceptional teacher of Art/Craft, who in the past had been encouraged to use her skills to teach *all* the Art and Crafts to half-classes in the upper school. Through workshops and staff discussion we began to share her experience and advice amongst the staff.

A measure of the success of this venture was that when she was seconded for a year to another school, the quality and variety of art-work generally in the school did not suffer to any real degree. Indeed, other teachers saw this opportunity as a challenge.

3. Provide brochures and inspection trips

These make use of external and internal stimuli to signal the possibility and direction of future change. External 'brochures' which I found helpful to present to my staff came from a variety of sources; they were mainly HMI and LEA publications such as *Better Schools*, *Education Observed 3 – Good Teachers*, and so on. At the same time we were beginning to consider our own policies and practices, and I was instrumental in providing documents as starting points – for example, in our consideration of the teaching of Environmental Studies throughout the school. This particular 'brochure' explained the reasons for reviewing this particular area of the curriculum, under the following general headings:

(a)   place in the curriculum;
(b)   aims;
(c)   status; prominence within a wide curriculum;
(d)   'open' learning;
(e)   from teaching to learning; a change of emphasis;
(f)   benefits – for learners, teachers, others;
(g)   learning materials and resources;
(h)   organization – optimum conditions;
(i)   skills and concepts;
(j)   our own scheme.

We have worked through all these stages in our staff meetings this year, with the intention of resolving the critical issues of continuity and record-keeping by the end of the Summer Term. The whole process has taken about 18 months, but this long, steady, deliberate progress has ensured the staff's full understanding and agreement.

Inspection trips were to institutions of a similar size and type to our own. The whole staff spent a day visiting a school, talking with Head, staff and children and then questioning what we could transfer or adapt to our own situation. The particular reason for this visit was to observe optimum use of an open-plan building, ease of access to staff expertise and resources, and the degree of responsibility vested in the children.

Some staff visited another school, where the focus was on the way work is honed and refined by individuals and groups of very ordinary children to produce finished articles of the most extraordinary quality and sensitivity.

Again, it is critical to recognize that the talents of individuals on one's own staff are celebrated and shared, and used as a stimulus for others through opportunities for paired teaching, classroom observation or workshop sessions. I was fortunate here in that the open-plan school allows teachers to see one another teaching. Paired teaching began with staff talking about the benefits of using remedial support *in* the classroom, extending this to using part-time staff for paired teaching, and the committed then convincing the doubters. I also taught alongside members of staff, explaining that I would simply help whenever I had the time, and being welcomed without reservation as an unobtrusive supporter/mentor within the classroom.

4. Plan the route

Notice first of all how late in the process we are giving attention to the direction of our endeavours. To maintain the school as a caring, sharing community it is vital that *all* of us engaged in this journey of discovery, learning and growth which I am describing here. Planning is a time-consuming exercise, and since the time any conscientious teacher can devote to meetings is basically for these planning meetings, all the more mundane issues vital to a school's health and well-being are relegated to brief lunchtime get-togethers as and when required. The full staff meetings before (8.00 a.m.) or after (3.45 p.m.) school last about one hour. The meetings held before school are often the more productive because people come fresh to them, and know there will be a time after registration when I take full assembly whilst the staff have some space to organize themselves for the busy day ahead. Occasionally the rigours of an even earlier start have been offset by the provision of a full English breakfast at school!

All such meetings are minuted by the individual members of staff in turn, and the minute book is then available for anyone who was ill or otherwise unable to attend the meeting. The purpose of this collaborative activity is to confirm and strengthen our commitment to the direction, pace and provisions necessary for a worthwhile journey.

5. Equip the team

This is another vital stage where too many well-intentioned plans lose their way. It is not enough simply to agree on what is required and then leave the staff to get on and provide it. There is a constant need for support, for advice, for encouragement and for praise. I find the monitoring role of the Head at its most valuable in this context. Equipping the staff has implications for time, resources and skills.

Some staff needed more time than others during any particular period of growth. This should come to be understood and respected by all, not envied or resented.

Spending was based on the present demands of staff and pupils, rather than apportioned to subject departments like slices of cake. Staff soon came to appreciate that this form of flexibility in finance and resource policy is a strength rather than a weakness.

The acquisition of new skills is critical because a willing staff can come to share common aims, but putting them into practice can place unacceptable demands on those who have had no opportunity to equip themselves with the necessary repertoire of teaching and learning strategies. These skills add to the teacher's talents, rather than being presented as compensating for past deficiencies.

Within GRIST (Grant Related In-service Training) funding my own Authority has asked each school for a written staff development policy; this was not any hardship in my case because of the way I am working *with* my staff jointly setting goals for the individuals and the team along the route of our journey.

Our priorities have been identified, agreed and approached. An example might be the place of school journeys within our Environmental Studies scheme. 'Firsthand experience is paramount wherever it is practical'. An early warning to me was the realization that it is not enough to discuss and agree such policies without ensuring that they are met in practice. The greatest doubts and reservations were held by long established teachers, or those with a limited repertoire of teaching/learning styles at their disposal. A great deal of advice and encouragement was needed before limited progress became apparent, and it would be realistic to admit that we still carry unwilling or uncertain travellers. Their caution can also be a benefit in the sense that they prevent our journey from becoming a headlong rush of over-enthusiasm. However, our scheme, based firmly on skills and concepts, was commended by HMI on a full inspection in 1987. That year, residential visits were offered to all four year-groups. All but one of the staff, and over 180 from a total of 260 pupils, participated in a range of well-planned and thoroughly educational visits.

6. Be prepared

Despite all the planning referred to above, I still found it necessary to be adaptable and prepared for various unexpected situations. Delays en-route will be encountered: industrial action over the prolonged pay dispute was a prime example here. However, because we all shared ownership of the enterprise and anticipated successful outcomes, the delay was only slight and of little real consequence.

There may be times when it is necessary to retrace one's step, as a constructive form of consolidation. This was found to be especially important upon the appointment of new members of staff.

Diversions from the planned route should be relatively few and far between. One that we encountered followed the HMI inspection, which was particularly critical of what they saw as the extraction and isolation of children with remedial needs. The problem was addressed as a matter of urgency, weighing the advantages and disadvantages of the way we currently operated before agreeing on a new format of special needs provision (which, incidentally, included exceptionally able children within its remit as well).

Short-cuts are a delight when they present themselves, though I would not actively seek them. After our first year of offering residential visits to all four year-groups, a teacher I envisaged saying, 'Never again!' said instead, 'When we go next year...'.

7. As you travel

'To be educated is not to have arrived, it is to travel with a different view'. The type of journey I have described has no absolute destination, no point of arrival, but many stations along the way where one can look back at the ground one has covered and refresh oneself for that which lies ahead. To stop for good, to suggest that the team has reached the ultimate goal, I would suggest is the beginning of stagnation for all concerned.

However, if the outlook is constantly varied and exciting, and the vehicle provides sufficient stability, the journey will be one of enjoyment, commitment and growth for all concerned.

Comment

This study is a sequential account of the steps involved in bringing about, gradually, major changes in the learning style in a school which, despite being physically open-plan, was in fact traditional in practice. The Head's objectives were clear in his own mind: a shift from teaching, especially class-teaching, to pupil learning; from teacher direction to greater pupil responsibility; and more individual and group learning. It is interesting that planning for longer-term objectives came late in the management sequences. The first item of any good management plan is: assess fully the existing circumstances. This the Head did in his first year as a new Head. His introduction of intended change then followed, not as precept, but as example: his own example in working with the existing arrangements. Directions of change came to be recognized by staff and accepted at least in theory: how to turn them into practice?

The Head gradually opened up the school to external and internal stimuli. Published material was supplemented by internal review of particular areas of the curriculum and the sharing of individual teachers' talents led to the spread of change. Visits to other schools were occasions for both give and take. At the late stage of planning ahead it was now possible to involve all the staff. The need for review of the provision and use of resources – human and material – became evident. Review of progress revealed the need for reconsideration and the recognition of fresh needs. As the Head concludes, there is no final destination.

Meanwhile the questions posed at the end of the study will have to be addressed, albeit by a well-integrated school community.

Questions for the reader's consideration

- The 'journey' described is largely about the *delivery* of the curriculum. Could or should (a) parents (b) governors be involved in any way in such a journey as is described in this study?

- In what ways should the constraints arising from the introduction of the National Curriculum and of assessment and testing under the ERA be met?

Commentary on case studies N to Q

The role of Headteacher

Among the many questions raised in our introductory chapter, those relating to the Headteacher's role and those concerned with relations with parents are well illuminated by our four contributors to this section. As in the previous section, the part played by governors is very little referred to (School P is an exception), and the role of the LEA only in the cases where a specific initiative has been taken or financially supported by the Authority. We intend later in this commentary to add our own comments on the role of governors. We begin, however, with the Head: administrator, manager, leader. Heads take it for granted that administrative procedures must be properly arranged and carefully followed. Head Q specifically notices the importance of good communication. Fortunately most primary schools are small enough for this to be largely personal; but it must not be left to chance meetings. The Head must accept final responsibility for seeing that administration is properly carried out, whether it be the dinner money or teacher punctuality.

We have explored the managerial role of the Head a good deal in the previous section. A particular aspect of good management brought out in more than one of the studies in this section is the way in which Heads have succeeded in getting teachers to adopt desirable changes in such a way as to feel what is tellingly referred to as 'shared ownership'. The journey described by Head Q presents a sequence of management behaviour which we find helpful and which bears many similarities to the one described in our first chapter. For this particular Head, the sequence is: where are we to start with? Lead by example; outside help; forward planning; resourcing; monitor and adapt as you go along.

All four of our contributors to this section are not simply managers. Each study brings out aspects of leadership. Head N looks carefully at her own role, the nature and extent of delegation, the reserve powers, as it were, of the Head, the importance of not having adopted too high a profile herself in the particular development described. The steps described by Head O in developing greater openness in the relations between parents and teachers bring out the importance of leadership and example. The Head has first to make sure she is open and accessible and has real contact with parents. She builds on the success of some teachers to encourage others and gives special help to some, such as probationary teachers, for whom greater parental contact might seem threatening. In the case of Head Q, the impression of positive leadership is strong: a clear recognition of the need for change and a perception of the direction in which it is required, namely towards pupil learning, albeit pursued in a journey of which gradualness is an important characteristic.

Parents

In three of the four studies, the Heads are describing the development of greater parental involvement. The first step is the accessibility to the Head and to the class-teacher. Deeper involvement comes with the growth of home reading arrangements and the chance for parents to understand more fully the learning experiences of their children by coming to class assemblies. Parents who only expect to hear if there is trouble are encouraged by hearing about success. Positive in-school help from parents is a feature of most primary schools but, of course, only a small minority of parents are involved. Heads recognize that there are many parents with whom the most desirable links cannot be sustained for practical reasons. Cooperation developed through frequent contact while mother is still at home is bound to falter when the youngest child becomes of school age and the mother goes out to work. In any case, from the school's point of view, the close involvement of parents of young children with the school is expected to diminish as the pupils gain greater independence. There is little or no mention of parents in the eight to 12 school study. Nevertheless, it is to be hoped that if a good foundation is laid in the early years, parents will still find teachers accessible in later years and that occasions for them to gain an understanding of curricular matters will be arranged.

The statutory duty laid on governors to reach decisions about sex education has led to greater parent and governor involvement in curricular decisions than has ever been the case before, as Head P describes. It is particularly important that in many schools, sex education has been discussed in the context of a much wider programme of personal, social and health education, over the whole field of which the Southampton/Exeter questionnaire ranged. The whole process of consultation about part of the curriculum described in this case study is a striking development which may prove to be a forerunner of increased consultation with both parents and governors about other areas of curriculum. The reconstitution of the governing bodies and their expected greater responsibilities under the Education Reform Act will be likely to lead in such a direction.

Governors

In our introductory chapter, we raised some questions about the role of governors to which our case studies have given very few answers. These studies were written after the 1986 Education Act and before the changes in the composition of governing bodies laid down under that Act had taken place. The Education Reform Act of 1988 was still on its way through Parliament. For the most part, the heads' relationships with governors were probably much as they had been in the past. Moreover the studies describe action taken over a period of years, up to early 1988. There were, with little doubt, many governing bodies under the old constitution on which governors as a whole played little part of any significance in the life of the school. They were involved, but infrequently, in the appointment of a Head or Deputy, though in the former case often overshadowed by members of the LEA and in receipt of officer/adviser advice. A few may have been involved occasionally in the appointment of assistant teachers. Beyond that, three shortish meetings a year, each largely devoted to listening to, asking questions about and commenting on the Head's report, made up the programme. In practice, Heads' attitudes towards governors have ranged over a spectrum of behaviour, at one end of which is that which prefers such minimal involvement. The Chairman of Governors in most cases played a more frequent part in the life of the school, visiting more often, consulting and being consulted by the Head, always involved in appointments and picking up from parents matters needing attention between meetings. In some cases, a real partnership between Head and chairman may, ironically, have reduced the role of other governors by virtue of problems having been foreseen or solved before the meeting.

But by the time our studies were actually written, the 1986 Act had already begun to change things. The responsibility upon governors to report annually to parents awakened governors appreciably. True, some Heads wrote the governors' report; but others, quite properly, said 'no' and the chairperson or someone else had to do it and get it approved. Though the attendance averaged, we hear, no more than 9 per cent of those eligible, many meetings were far from dull. As the changes laid down in the Education Reform Act come into effect, governors may well find themselves called to account by a greater number of concerned parents.

Under the 1988 Act, the new constitution of governing bodies will, in our view, present a challenge and an opportunity to Heads. We range ourselves strongly in support of that end of the spectrum of Head-behaviour in relation to governors which prefers, to quote an earlier phrase, the 'maximum degree of involvement [of governors] consistent with the final managerial responsibility [of the Head] for the effective functioning of the school'. There are more parent governors to be involved than before and there are governors co-opted for their special interest and background. Along with the fewer LEA nominees and the teachers' respresentatives, such a governing body, if well advised, encouraged and well-led, can be the means of bringing to bear wide support from the community which the school serves.

What has happened so far? The co-opted governors have been chosen at a first meeting attended by parent-governors, a similar number of LEA-nominated governors and the teacher-governors, including the Head, if he or she has chosen to become a governor. The fully completed governing body has begun to consider the best ways in which to meet their responsibilities under the new Act, especially in relation to the National Curriculum, to the assessment of pupils' progress and to the delegation of almost the whole financial responsibility for the school to the governors, except for schools with under 200 pupils (and not necessarily all of those). Advice has been forthcoming about the setting up of sub-committees able to deal respectively with finance, premises, staffing and the curriculum. Some important management issues merit examination and careful consideration by Heads.

The Local Education Authority

The Head will do well to consider afresh his relations with the LEA, its officers and advisers. In the small Primary Schools not given full financial delegation the interplay of relations between the Head, the governors and the Authority's officers over the critical matter of staffing will remain. The Head will still have to make a judgement from time to time as to how far to pursue a path of persuasion and negotiation with 'the office' or at what point to seek to bring pressure to bear from his governors. With fewer LEA nominees on the governing body, officers may find it easier to resist such pressure – who knows? When the great majority of the LEA's education budget has been shared out among the schools, the margin left at the centre will be small. Alongside this, all Primary Schools, including the smallest, will be directly affected by other parts of the new Act, notably the introduction of the National Curriculum. While in the larger schools the degree of self-government will be very nearly complete, this will be subject to the responsibility to satisfy the LEA that proper standards are being reached and financial resources properly used. The Head will do well to recognize not only this ultimate authority of the LEA but also the support and help which officers and advisers/inspectors can give. Information and advice of a confidential nature in relation to staff appointments, teaching and some non-teaching, will remain invaluable. Professional advice of other kinds will still be needed. Very exceptionally, this might arise if a Head found him- or herself in severe disagreement with the governing body.

Finance

It seems likely that LEAs may provide some special training for Heads in financial management. Heads will do well to assess existing financial resources along the lines suggested in case study M. They may wish to begin monitoring expenditure on such items as heating and lighting, minor repairs, telephone charges before full financial delegation begins. Restrictions on charging parents for certain pupil activities may have to be examined carefully and may call for a reconsideration of policy for some aspects of the curriculum. In larger schools, where money allocated for teachers' salaries will be on the basis of average salaries, it will be helpful at an early stage to establish the current cost of existing staff. The critical examination of current spending on 'capitation items', described in studies in Section 3, will be an on-going requirement.

Head/staff/governor relations

Our case studies continually bring out Heads' belief that changes can only satisfactorily be carried out on the basis of a consensus among the staff and with the Head. Under full financial delegation, this will be critically important and in many cases, such as the importance of keeping down costs of heating and lighting, for example, must include non-teaching staff. The role of teacher-governors needs careful thought. It is true that this role has already developed from past experience, but with the very much greater powers and responsibilities of governors under the Education Reform Act, this role may be subject to greater stresses than have so far occurred. The Head will be unwise to include in his report to the governors proposals which have not been discussed with the staff. He may well wish to sound out governors about a proposed development, without at this stage either having gained the full consensus of the staff or indeed reached his own final conclusion. A teacher-governor may well take an opportunity to oppose the Head's views and to seek governors' support for such a view. How far is it good management for the professionals to appear at odds before the laymen? There are notorious examples from the past of such a situation.

Membership of sub-committees is a matter which may well exercise the teacher-governors in particular. The most critical decisions seem likely to be made initially by the finance sub-committee, for the budget may well involve hard choices between expenditure on teachers, non-teaching staff and teaching materials. We would expect a teacher-governor to be a member of this sub-committee. A staff sub-committee presents a problem. On the face of it, we might expect a teacher here also. But in practice, this sub-committee will be largely concerned with selection and promotion of staff. Any decision in a Primary School about an incentive allowance affects, if only negatively, most other members of staff. Even a new appointment may well have to be made against the need, recognized by the Head, for a teacher who can help to overcome a weakness in one or another area of the curriculum. Here again a teacher-governor might need to declare an interest or indeed the Head wish to be able to confide in the governors in the absence of other teachers.

We take it for granted that the Head will be a member of, or attend, all sub-committees. That dealing with premises offers a good opportunity for direct cooperation between Head, a teacher-governor and one or more laymen, who hopefully may have some expertise to offer – especially if co-options have been well made! It is a question whether a single curriculum committee will work well. Certainly in this context, the Head and the teacher-governors belong, as it were, with the professionals in helping other governors to understand more about method and content, in relation to the National Curriculum. If, as we have indicated earlier, each teacher has a role within the curriculum which goes beyond and deeper than that of the class-teacher, then each should have direct contact with at least some of the governors in relation to a particular curriculum area. There is much to be said for, say, four small groups of governors to be constituted, each concerned with one of the four broad areas of language, Maths and Science, the Humanities and the Creative Arts. Such an arrangement might well suit plans, such as some of those described in the case studies, to review development in one area of the curriculum at a time.

Sub-committees, it must be assumed, will report back to full governors' meetings. It will be wise to be clear from the outset about the extent of a sub-committee's power to make decisions – for example in making appointments, or in other cases – for example the budget – to make considered recommendations to the full governing body. The Head will wish to consider who should do the actual reporting and in what form. This is a matter clearly in which the chairman of governors will be very much concerned.

The role of the chairperson of governors

Heads have plenty of experience of working with their past and present chairpersons. The question worth some consideration in the changing circumstances arising from the Education Reform Act is whether the chairperson's role needs to change or at least to be reconsidered. One aspect of this is the possibility of the vice-chairperson taking on a specific role and responsibility, say for one or two of the sub-committees. Should the chairperson be a member of all sub-committees – or indeed, of none? The latter arrangement would in time drastically alter the Head/chairperson relationship, as gradually many decisions would be taken and important reports prepared to the whole governing body in his absence. Probably, most chairpersons will wish to be involved at least in the staff and finance sub-committees. Heads will wish to consider how far they wish to continue to have a close link with the chairperson outside the more structured arrangements for the working of the governing body which seem sure to develop. They may recognize that there is a particular kind of leadership role which the chairperson may usefully play in coordinating the involvement of members of the governing body.

The Head's role in changing circumstances

The Head's role as chief professional must clearly be maintained, but exercised in such a way as to allow the maximum involvement of the governors in making the decisions which are within their responsibility. The role of the Head as manager will undoubtedly be enlarged as financial delegation comes into effect and Heads will wish to develop their own skills and perhaps to buy in special skills, possibly on a part-time basis, from other professionals. In all areas which will have become the governors' responsibility, the Head will remain the chief executive, answerable to the governing body as a managing director is to the board of directors. The Head's leadership role is more important than ever in these changing times: one who can be alongside colleagues, part of a consensus; one who takes initiatives and encourages others to do so as well; one who brings a wide vision of the school's role in the community as a whole; one able to help others to overcome weaknesses and is prepared to recognize his/her own.

Some Concluding Observations

In our general introduction to the case studies, we referred to three themes underlying our understanding of the essential nature of the headship role: leadership, management and changing external relations. In a sense, leadership and management skills are inextricably interrelated aspects of a single role, that of the Headteacher. But not only of the Headteacher, for these qualities are called for from all teachers, within whatever more limited framework they are given the opportunity to exercise them. In the case studies we have seen examples of strong leadership associated with developing arrangements involving the participation of all members of staff in consultation about curriculum change and the use of resources. Staff development and the introduction of job descriptions defining teachers' beyond-class responsibilities are extending the managerial role of the individual teacher beyond the traditional class-teaching role, in which the exercise of management skills was restricted to the single class.

Radical changes in the distribution of powers and responsibilities between central government, the Local Education Authorities and the individual schools are taking place as a result of the 1986 Education Act and the Education Reform Act 1988. On the one hand, the introduction of the National Curriculum and arrangements for the assessment and testing of pupils, together with the determination of the pay and conditions of service of teachers by central government, represent a powerful shift of powers to the national level. On the other hand, the increased powers and duties of school governing bodies, especially the coming introduction of local financial management together with the statutory arrangements for parent participation, represent an equally important shift towards the local level of the school itself. The variety of changes described in our case studies have in many cases put in place or have begun to put in place management arrangements which these national changes would have required in any case. Schools are already engaged on the task of delivering the National Curriculum and of developing pupil-profiling in accordance with the requirement for internal assessments and testing at 7, 11 and 14. Better arrangements for ensuring the best use of resources within pre-ERA circumstances, described in some of the studies, are a good introduction to the wider responsibilities under LMS when the school budget must cover almost all the direct expenditure of the school.

It is time perhaps to remind ourselves what it is all for. The objective of management, in whatever sphere, is to improve the product and to meet the customer's requirements. In simple terms, good school management is for the children. Many of our studies and our own commentaries have in fact made little mention of the children and, given the themes of these studies, this is quite understandable. But it is perhaps salutary to remind ourselves that the object of the enterprise is to provide every pupil with the best possible learning experiences. These experiences necessarily relate to the physical, social, intellectual and aesthetic environments in which they take place. Each of these aspects of the learning environment will now be even more fully under the control of the school than it has ever been before and this is the challenge to leadership and management in every school. The price of failure is boredom. The reward of success is lively and interested pupils.

Alongside the provision of worthwhile and enjoyable learning experiences for the children is the equally important requirement that pupils should achieve their maximum potential in the acquisition of skills, understanding and knowledge. It may be that the assessment and testing to be associated with the National Curriculum will place increased pressure on schools to assess their own success and to subject the decisions and changes made, of whatever kinds, to critical evaluation. It is greatly to be hoped that, in seeking success in what might be called the achievement aspects of the curriculum, the attainment targets, there will be no reduction in the quality of the learning experience of the child. For in the end, the quality of his or her development – personal, social, intellectual, aesthetic – will depend more than anything on what it has been like, for him or her, to have been a pupil in the class and the school at the time.

Bibliography

A list of sources relating to management which readers may find of use

ADAIR, J. (1985). *Effective Decision Making*. London: Pan Books.

ADAIR, J. (1988). *Effective Leadership*. London: Pan Books.

BAILEY, A.J. (1987). *Support for School Management*. London: Croom Helm.

BASTIANI, J. (Ed.) (1987). *Parents and Teachers: Perspectives on Home–School Relations*. Windsor: NFER-NELSON.

BASTIANI, J. (Ed.) (1988a). *Parents and Teachers: 2. From Policy to Practice*. Windsor: NFER-NELSON.

BASTIANI, J. (Ed.) (1988b). *Parents and Teachers: 3. Working with Parents*. Windsor: NFER-NELSON.

BECHER, T. and ERAUT, M. (1981). *Policies for Educational Accountability*. Oxford: Heinemann.

BELL, L. (1988). *Management Skills in Primary Schools*. London: Routledge.

CIPFA (Chartered Institute of Public Finance and Accountancy). (1988). *Local Management in Schools*. London: LMS Initiative.

CRAIG, I. (Ed.) (1987). *Primary School Management in Action*. Harlow, Essex: Longman.

CRAIG, I. (Ed.) (1989). *Primary Headship in the 1990s*. Harlow, Essex: Longman.

CULLINGFORD, C. (1985). *Parents, Teachers and Schools*. London: Robert Royce.

DAY, C. (1985). *Managing Primary Schools*. London: Harper and Row.

DAY, C., WHITAKER, P. and WREN, D. (1987). *Appraisal and Professional Development in Primary Schools*. Milton Keynes: Open University.

DEAN, J. (1987). *Managing the Primary School*. London: Croom Helm.

GLATTER, R. *et al.* (1988). *Understanding School Management*. Milton Keynes: Open University.

HARDING, P. (1987). *A Guide to Governing Schools*. London: Harper and Row.

HERSEY, P. and BLANCHARD, K. (1982). *Management of Organisational Behaviour*. (4th edition). Hemel Hempstead, Herts: Prentice Hall.

HEWTON, E. (1988a). *The Appraisal Interview*. Milton Keynes: Open University.

HEWTON, E. (1988b). *School Focussed Staff Development*. London: Falmer.

HOYLE, E. (1986). *The Politics of School Management*. Sevenoaks, Kent: Hodder and Stoughton.

MCCORMICK, R. and JAMES, M. (1983). *Curriculum Evaluation in Schools*. London: Croom Helm.

MURPHY, R. and TORRANCE, R. (1987). *Evaluating Education*. London: Paul Chapman.

PAISEY, A. and M. (1987). *Effective Management in Primary Schools*. Oxford: B. Blackwell.

SALLIS, J. (1988). *Schools, Parents and Governors*. London: Routledge.

SOUTHGATE, G. (1987). *Readings in Primary Schools Management*. London: Falmer.

Journals from NFER-NELSON

TOPIC – PRACTICAL APPLICATIONS OF RESEARCH IN EDUCATION

All too often a yawning gap seems to exist between educational research and classroom practice. TOPIC, a new resource pack from NFER-NELSON, has been specifically designed to bridge that gap. It draws out the practical implications for teachers, lecturers, advisers and students of a wide range of the latest research findings.

Published twice yearly in the Spring and Autumn, TOPIC has a looseleaf format so that it can conveniently be photocopied for group discussions, staff meetings and in-house training. With its short articles and reports it is an ideal way for education practitioners to keep up to date with the latest research as it affects their daily work.

Educational Research

Educational Research is the termly journal of the NFER, Britain's leading research institute in the educational field.

Drawing on projects in universities, colleges of education, and other institutions in Britain, the journal aims to disseminate research findings at all levels of education from policy making to classroom teaching.

Articles include a wide variety of research studies and reviews of research, summaries of research findings in more specialised fields, and comprehensive reviews of new books in the field of research on education generally. In addition the latest projects carried out by the NFER are summarised.

Published in February, June and November.

The European Journal of Special Needs Education

Published in response to the need in this area for a journal that moves beyond the confines of conventional research-based articles, the *European Journal of Special Needs Education* presents studies, reports and information of international significance. Launched in 1986 the journal continues to grow and develop and will appeal to teachers, advisers and students as well as researchers.

Published in March, June and October.

Research Papers in Education

Research Papers in Education is a unique forum for high quality research papers in all fields of education.

The journal builds up a library of empirical work that does not fit easily into conventional article or book format. Each issue tackles current topics in a lively and informative style.

Published in March, June and October.

For sample copies and/or subscription details contact:

International Thomson Publishing Services Ltd., North Way, Andover, Hampshire, SP10 5BE.

NFER-NELSON · Darville House · 2 Oxford Road East
Windsor · Berkshire · SL4 1DF
Tel: (0753) 858961   Fax: (0753) 856830

HOTLINE   Tel: (0753) 858600